D0478458

FROM THE BOOKS OF

Campbell

Shrines of Power

The Grand Tour

Shrines of Power

Flavio Conti

Translated by Patrick Creagh

HBJ Press

Boston

HBJ Press

President, Robert J. George

Publisher, Giles Kemp

Vice President, Richard S. Perkins, Jr.

Managing Director, Valerie S. Hopkins

Text Director, Marcia Heath

Text Editors: Elizabeth R. DeWitt, Karen E. English, Carolyn Hall, Peggy Wagner, Gregory Weed

Editorial Staff: Betsie Brownell, Karen Fraser, Ann McGrath, Nancy Knoblock, Janet Schotta

Project Coordinator, Linda S. Behrens

Architectural Consultant, Dennis J. DeWitt

Project Consultant, Ann S. Moore

Design Implementation, Designworks

Rizzoli Editore

Authors of the Italian Edition: Jiri Burian, Dr. Flavio Conti, Henri Stierlin, Jersy Szablowski, Dr. Gian Maria Tabarelli

Idea and Realization, Harry C. Lindinger

General Supervisor, Luigi U. Re

Graphic Designer, Gerry Valsecchi

Coordinator, Vilma Maggioni

Editorial Supervisor, Gianfranco Malafarina

Research Organizer, Germano Facetti

U.S. Edition Coordinator, Natalie Danesi Murray

Photography Credits:

Hassmann: pp. 57, 60–68/ *Michael Holford:* pp. 105, 106–107, 108, 109 top left & bottom right, 110–112, 113 bottom left, 114 top left & right, 115 top left & right, 116/ *Klammet & Aberl:* pp. 58–59, 138–139/ *Magnum-T. Takahara:* pp. 121–130, 131 top & center, 132/ *Mauritius:* p. 115 bottom/ *Oronoz:* pp. 12–16, 17 top left & right, 19–20, 22–23, 25 bottom left & right, 26 bottom left & right, 28 top left & center right, 29/ *V. Radnicky:* pp. 137, 140–148/ *Rivas-Salmer:* p. 9/ *Rizzoli:* pp. 73, 74–75, 76 center left & bottom left, 78 top, 79 top, 131 bottom left & right/ *Scala:* pp. 41–48, 49 bottom, 50 left, 51–52, 76 top left & right, 76 center right, 77, 78 bottom left & right, 79 bottom, 80–96/ *Scala-Bencini:* pp. 153–164/ *Sheridan:* 49 top, 50 bottom right, 109 top right, 114 bottom left/ *Henri Stierlin:* p. 113 top left, right, center right & bottom right/ *Zerkowitz:* pp. 10–11, 17 bottom, 18, 21, 24, 26 top, 27, 28 bottom left, 30–32.

© 1977 by Rizzoli Editore-International Division
Copyright © 1978 by HBJ Press, Inc.

All rights reserved. No part of this publication may be reproduced or transmitted in any form or by any means, electronic or mechanical, including photocopy, recording, or any information storage and retrieval system, without permission in writing from the publisher.

Library of Congress Catalog Card Number: 77–908–63
ISBN: 0-15-003725-2

Printed in Hong Kong by Mandarin Publishers Limited

Contents

The Alhambra, Spain 9

The Roman Forum, Italy 41

Heidelberg Castle, West Germany 57

St. Peter's, Vatican City 73

Temple of Amon, Egypt 105

The Imperial Palace, Japan 121

The Binnenhof, the Netherlands 137

Edinburgh Castle, Scotland 153

Preface

Shrines of Power

Through the ages, the major problem confronting architects has not been designing beautiful buildings but rather financing them. Frank Lloyd Wright, the greatest American architect of the twentieth century, was once asked by his students what—above all—they should do to become good architects. Wright's answer was succinct: "Find good clients." Of course, he was right. A wealthy, discriminating, intelligent patron is a key prerequisite to a successful building. The architect, unlike the painter, cannot do his work first and sell it afterward. He must first have a client with substantial financial means and clear-cut needs. Therefore, architecture is the product of two forces—the genius and inspiration of the architect and the demands and resources of influential patrons. It is not surprising then that architectural masterpieces—even today— have long been regarded as sanctuaries of prestige and authority. Those with the most power could afford the highest prices and could therefore commission the best architects to design and build for them. The works they commissioned usually served as a proclamation of their exalted stature and were intended to immortalize their fame in wood and stone.

Shrines of Power is a journey of discovery through eight groups of buildings in places as widespread as Europe, Africa, and Asia. These religious, regal, and political strongholds belong to diverse eras, and their forms and styles are as varied as the cultures which inspired them. The castles at Heidelberg and Edinburgh, the Alhambra, and the Imperial Palace at Kyoto were all built to enhance the authority of those who ruled from within their walls— through their splendor, elegance, and elaborate fortifications. On the other hand, the Basilica of St. Peter's in Rome and the Temple of Amon at Karnak speak of a different kind of power: the power of religion. Finally, there are the centers of political powers: the Binnenhof, a symbol of the United Provinces of the Netherlands, and the Roman Forum, an open space in a once marshy valley that eventually came to epitomize Roman cultural dominance.

But these sanctuaries of power do more than merely remind us of the names of the architects who created them or the wealth and influence of those who commissioned them. They reflect the human emotions and experiences, the political conflicts, and the religious devotions which transpired within their walls. They eloquently embody history, endowing it with life and form.

Among these sanctuaries of power is the red sandstone castle of Heidelberg. Originally a medieval fortress, the castle was later established as the seat of the electors Palatine. By the fifteenth century, it was a flourishing haven for artists, writers, and philosophers. During the seventeenth century, however, Heidelberg Castle was twice taken and battered by the armies of Louis XIV, and a century later it was struck by lightning. Today, many of its Gothic, Renaissance, and baroque buildings still stand—shattered but strikingly beautiful.

The Temple of Amon at Karnak has also suffered from the passage of time, with its ebb and flow of conquerors and, at times, of whole cultures. But these ruins on the banks of the Nile have not lost their original majesty and poetry. Napoleon Bonaparte, in his abortive Egyptian colonial adventure, signaled Europe's reawakened awareness of the vast and impressive monuments of this ancient culture. It is fitting that one of his officers happened to find the Rosetta stone, one of the most important archaeological discoveries of all time and the key to our study of ancient Egypt. Because of the Rosetta stone, the delicate sculptures carved in Karnak's sun-baked desert walls once more reveal the sovereignty and military conquests of pharaohs who worshipped there more than three thousand years ago.

The story of Rome, like that of Karnak, also spans many millenniums. As Karnak's strength and influence faded, Rome's Forum was fast becoming the bustling, thriving hub of a city that was to be the center of the Western civilized world. From the Forum, roads radiated out toward far-flung provinces. Here, the victorious generals—Septimius Severus, Sulla, Caesar, and Pompey—returned in triumph; here, Saint Peter came to preach a gospel, which was then spread to the rest of the world. Today, the Roman Empire has passed, and only the marble fragments of the Forum hint at its former strength.

The glory of Renaissance Rome lives on, however, in St. Peter's Basilica, whose conception and construction involved so many of the finest Renaissance artists. The dome of St. Peter's, symbol of the Vatican city-state, is best known as the work of Michelangelo. However, it was actually constructed after the architect's death, and the proportions of his design were so greatly modified that it was finally necessary to encircle it with an iron chain to prevent it from bursting apart. Ironically enough, the financing of St. Peter's—a sublime, daring monument to the enduring strength and power of Christianity—led Martin Luther to draw up his Ninety-five Theses of Wittenberg, which caused the definitive schism within the Western church.

The Imperial Palace at Kyoto in Japan dates back to the eighth century. For generations, it was the residence of the emperors. Its fragile wooden buildings were often ravaged by fire, but their serene sense of timeless continuity and atmosphere remains unspoiled. The power of the Japanese emperors was transferred at an early date to the samurai and the shoguns, but their palace, with its tea pavilions and bamboo fences set among graceful gardens, ponds, and trees, is still one of the finest jewels of Japanese architecture.

The beautiful palace–fortress of the Alhambra in Spain has housed rulers and conquerors as different as the Moorish kings of the Nasrid dynasty; Ferdinand and Isabella; and Holy Roman Emperor Charles V. Standing proudly on a rocky plateau in the Sierra Nevada, the original ninth-century fortress gradually evolved into a luxurious Islamic palace of open courtyards, refreshing gardens, and bubbling fountains, surrounded by elegant plaster arcades ornamented with intricate abstract and floral patterns. Charles V loved the Alhambra, yet he tore down part of it to build his own palace. The striking contrast of its solid, Renaissance design with the fluid lines of the Moorish palace reveals how differently architecture can be used to express personal power and cultural dominance.

Another monument of power is Edinburgh Castle, symbolizing the fortitude of the Scottish monarchy and Scottish pride and resistance during the nation's unremitting struggles against the English. The center of Scotland's turbulent history, rich mythology, and proud traditions, its ancient halls have been the backdrop for many dark and bloody scenes, and its name is linked with the dramatic stories of Macbeth and Malcolm, Robert the Bruce, and the tragic Mary Queen of Scots.

The Binnenhof in The Hague knew little of the stormy violence that marked the history of Edinburgh. It was the inner court of a castle that the counts of Holland had built during the Middle Ages on the windswept dunes of the Dutch coast. But toward the end of the sixteenth century, it became the seat of the States-General of the United Provinces of the Netherlands, a symbol of Dutch autonomy against the despotic power of Philip II of Spain. Most of the original Gothic and Romanesque buildings have disappeared and have been replaced by the quiet rectangle of refined, reserved seventeenth-century dark brick palaces—now legislative and administrative buildings—which surround the restored medieval Hall of Knights.

These eight different monuments record the power of individuals, governments, cultures, and ideals—both religious and national. Though some have endured the ravages of time and violence better than others, none retains the temporal power it once commanded. Yet as symbols of strength, they continue to appeal to the imagination, re-creating the lives of those who built and inhabited them, and thus triumphing over time as their creators might have wished.

The Alhambra

Spain

Preceding page, a general view of the Alhambra. Though the walls of the Alhambra may seem impregnable, set on a high, outlying plateau of the snow-capped Sierra Nevada, they were never actually tested in battle. In 1492, the conquering sovereigns, Ferdinand and Isabella, signaled their bloodless capture of Granada by raising the cross and royal standards on the massive Torre de la Vela at far right.

Above, the Torre de los Picos on the northern walls. This tower appears as it did in the thirteenth and fourteenth centuries, but other parts of the walls have changed entirely. Such is the case with the Tower of the Ladies (left), with a mirador *that affords a panoramic view of Granada and the surrounding countryside.*

Facing page, the roofs of the Alhambra. The configuration of glazed tile roofs provides an idea of the layout, which is ordered but complex and varied. The arcade of the Court of the Lions can be seen in the distance. In the foreground are the domes of the baths with their myriad skylights that appear starlike from the inside.

One of the two principal courts, the Court of the Myrtles (above) is dominated by the large reflecting pool. Water was everywhere in the Alhambra. To the Moors, it was as important a material as brick, stone, or wood in the construction of a suitable dwelling. In this inner court, built during the reign of Yusuf I, the architect's use of water gives an impression of spiritual peace and beauty.

Facing page, the portico of the Court of the Myrtles—with its arcade of slender, white marble columns and intricately carved plaster arches.

From the outside, a visitor would never guess at the beauty within. The Alhambra's walls, towers, and exterior gateways, such as the Gate of Wine (far left) and the Gate of Justice (left), seem almost austere when compared to the lavish decoration of the interior.

The additions of Christian kings and their successors can be seen throughout the Alhambra, as in the Fountain of Charles V (above) and the reconstructed Garden of Daraxa (right). Christians are in fact responsible for much more than appears at first sight, but the palace overwhelmingly retains its Islamic identity. The Gardens of the Partal (below) are essentially a modern reconstruction in the Islamic spirit: a harmonious arrangement of water, vegetation, and architecture.

The Tower of the Ladies (facing page) has a terrace with a five-arched mirador, which overlooks the city. Restored in the nineteenth century, it was originally built during the reign of Yusuf I (1333–1354).

Facing page, the Court of the Lions, the most celebrated part of the Alhambra. Here, the royal family could walk in complete privacy. Built at the time of Mohammed V, it was designed around twelve, water-spouting marble lions that encircle a large, alabaster fountain.

Above, the pavilion on the western side of the court, and below, a sunlit colonnade adjoining it.

The fantastic patterns of carved, geometric designs shown here, both abstract and floral, reached the peak of refinement and beauty in the Court of the Lions.

Among the most inventive features of Muslim architecture are the inlaid wood and stalactite plaster decorations (right) that hang from the vaulted ceilings of the Alhambra. The cupola of the Hall of the Abencerrajes (below and below right) is honeycombed with innumerable cells that seem to be exploding outward and downward. But the most famous example is the stalactite decoration (following page) found in the Hall of the Two Sisters.

Adjacent to the Lion and Myrtle courts, the courtyard of the Palace of Charles V (above) reflects a contrasting artistic temperament. The palace, begun in 1526 by the architect Machuca, displays a bold symmetric design, characteristic of Italian Renaissance architecture, unlike the subtle interwoven shapes and patterns that typify the Islamic. Compare the courtyard of Charles's palace with the Hall of the Ambassadors (facing page), the oratory (below) just off the Mexuar, and the Cuarto Dorado (below right).

The Nasrid kings of the Alhambra gave audience to their subjects in the Mexuar (above), completed in 1365.

Left, details of the capitals. The delicate ornamentation and slenderness of the columns provide a sharp architectural contrast to the massiveness of the piers, crossbeams, and ceiling.

The Mirador of Daraxa (above) is located on a second-story hallway off the Hall of the Two Sisters. This balcony, the garden it faces, and the adjoining apartments are reputed to have been used chiefly by Lindaraja, a favorite queen.

Left, an entrance leading into the Hall of the Ambassadors. The calligraphy that surrounds the doorway is masterfully integrated with the geometric ornamentation. The interior is partially decorated with ceramic tile.

The Hall of the Baths was built during the reign of Yusuf I. Although the tiles are crumbling in the principal bath as well as in a number of the other stone tubs, the resting room of the baths (shown on this page) is in remarkable condition. The two-story structure is lit by windows (below) high above the marble floor.

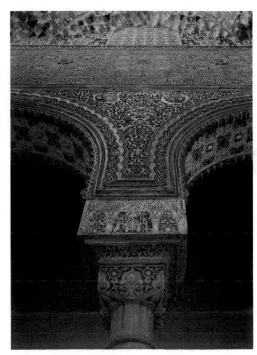

A characteristic architectural motif of the Al-hambra is its elaborate archways. The series of arches in the Hall of Justice (preceding page) and the assemblage of arches shown on this page attest to the immense vitality of the Moorish artists and architects. The arched *miradores* (facing page and following page), as well as the variously designed and decorated arches and interior gateways, unify the Alhambra and temper the complexity of its organization.

The Alhambra, Spain

For almost eight hundred years, the Spanish Christians had struggled to reconquer their land from the Moors—Muslims from northern Africa who had first invaded Spain in the early eighth century. On January 2, 1492, in Granada, the Catholic sovereigns, Ferdinand of Aragon and Isabella of Castile, received the long-awaited surrender of the last Muslim ruler on Spanish soil. To proclaim their victory, Cardinal Mendoza, Count Tendilla, and the Master of the Order of Santiago raised a silver cross and the royal standards of Aragon and Castile on the Torre de la Vela, the largest of the Alhambra's towers.

And with the Muslim defeat, one of the world's great architectural treasures—the Alhambra—fell into Spanish hands. Constructed principally during the thirteenth and fourteenth centuries, the Alhambra is a palace-fortress set on an outlying plateau of the Sierra Nevada overlooking Granada. The group of buildings—designed and ornamented by Moorish artists—housed, protected, and graced the lives of the kings of the Nasrid dynasty.

The architectural beauty of the Alhambra evolved from humble beginnings. In the late ninth century, the Moors hastily erected a small, plain fortress to protect themselves from the recurrent peasant uprisings. This fortress, known as the Alcazába, had pinkish walls, and it was this color that gave the Alhambra its name, for *al-hamrá* means "the red" in Arabic. The Alcazába soon came to be referred to as *Al-Qal'a al-Hamrá,* the Red Fortress.

Today, the walls of the Alcazába and the Alhambra—many of them now stuccoed or surfaced in a primitive form of concrete—stand like a rocky outcrop on the crest of the hill, aloof from the whitewashed walls of the modern city below. Historically insignificant itself, the Alcazába was the seed of both the Alhambra's name and its architectural growth.

The Moors of Granada chose well when they decided to build on the Sabika—a high, rocky plateau that was a spur of the Sierra Nevada. A natural citadel, the hill had in fact been fortified centuries earlier, first by the Iberians and later by the Romans, and on these ancient foundations the Moors built their Alcazába.

The Moors had controlled Spain almost from the moment in 711 when Tarik ibn Ziyad set foot on one of the two great rocks that marked the boundary between Africa and Europe. Today, that rock is called Gibraltar, a name derived from *Jebel-al-Tarik,* or Mountain of Tarik. From there, Tarik and his Muslim army swept through Spain, easily toppling the decaying kingdom of the Visigoth, Roderick. It was a conquest of faith because the Moors—who were converted to Islam in the early eighth century, thus becoming Muslims—were filled with the fire of their new religion.

Muslim conquerors were already entrenched throughout the formerly Christian lands of the Near East and North Africa. Their strength posed a threat to all

Below, the Alhambra and environs as it appeared after the Christian Reconquest.

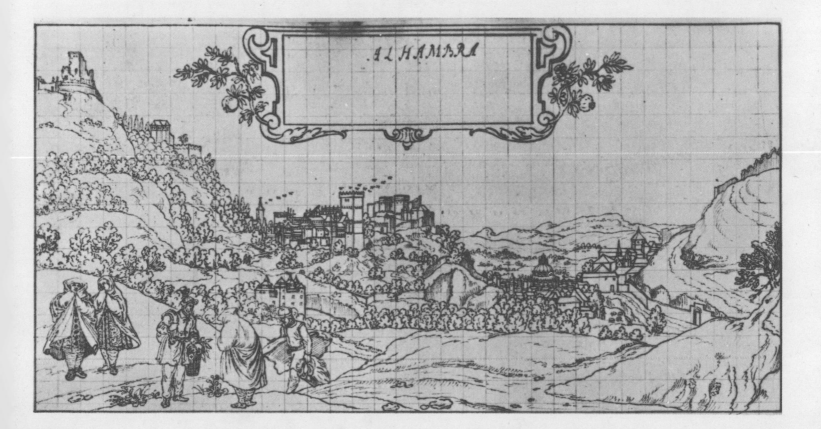

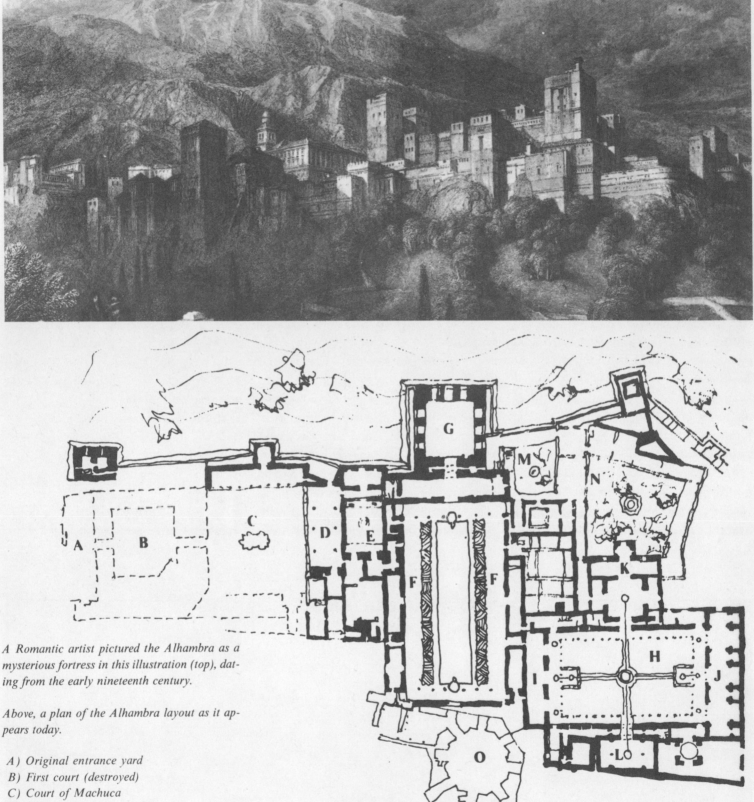

A Romantic artist pictured the Alhambra as a mysterious fortress in this illustration (top), dating from the early nineteenth century.

Above, a plan of the Alhambra layout as it appears today.

A) *Original entrance yard*
B) *First court (destroyed)*
C) *Court of Machuca*
D) *Mexuar*
E) *Court of the Cuarto Dorado*
F) *Court of the Myrtles*
G) *Hall of the Ambassadors*
H) *Court of the Lions*
I) *Hall of the Mocárabes*
J) *Hall of Justice (or Hall of the Kings)*
K) *Mirador of Daraxa*
L) *Hall of the Abencerrajes*
M) *Court of the Grate*
N) *Garden of Daraxa*
O) *Chapel of the Palace of Charles V*

of Western Europe. But the Frankish king, Charles Martel, turned the Muslim tide at the Battle of Poitiers in 732 and so became a national hero and the progenitor of an imperial family.

Nevertheless, Spain had been won, and the Moors and their culture were to remain there for nearly eight centuries.

During most of this time, the small Alcazába of Granada remained sufficient to defend and control the city—even in the eleventh century, when Granada grew to be the center of one of the small ephemeral kingdoms that resulted from the fragmentation of the Umayyad dynasty of Córdoba. Not until 1238, when the Nasrid dynasty of Granada gained control of Moorish Spain, did the Alcazába become inadequate for the city's defense. The Reconquest—the name given to the struggle of the Spanish Christians to repossess the country—had by this time limited the area of Moorish control to Andalusia in the extreme south of Spain. In 1212, the Christians had won a landmark victory at the strategic mountain town of Las Navas de Tolosa, and by 1236, Ferdinand III of Castile had ousted the Moors from Córdoba. The natural capital of the territory remaining under Moorish control was Granada, near the foot of the Sierra Nevada, the mountains which divided Muslim Andalusia from the threatening Spanish Catholic armies.

For another two and a half centuries, the Moors under the Nasrid dynasty held on valiantly in this region. Here, amid a civilization in retreat, the finest expression of Islamic architecture in Europe was born—the Alhambra. Although Moorish power in Spain was declining, the Nasrids nevertheless built a palace so magnificent that the court poet ibn Zamrack was inspired to write the lines now engraved over one of the gateways:

> Give me charity, lady,
> for there is nothing in life
> like the pain of being a blind man
> in Granada.

Decorative inscriptions, such as the ones on the right from the Court of the Lions, appear throughout the Alhambra complex.

Below, a representation of the surrender of Granada to the Catholic sovereigns, Ferdinand of Aragon and Isabella of Castile, in 1492. The final Moorish defeat was bloodless, and it marked the conclusion of the Christian Reconquest of Spain, which had begun in 1085.

An Islamic Treasure in Europe

The first Nasrid king, Mohammed I, was more concerned with securing the decaying Alcazába than in creating a beautiful palace. Coming to the throne in the spring of 1238, he immediately set about this task and also ordered the construction of aqueducts to bring in water from the mountains. The introduction of water to the Alcazába proved to be a significant achievement not only for obvious practical reasons but also for aesthetic ones. Tranquil pools, tinkling fountains, flowering

gardens, and lush green vegetation would all be fundamental to the design and appeal of the Alhambra.

Mohammed II completed the work of his father in fortifying the Alcazába; he added new bulwarks, ramparts, and imposing towers. He also began construction of the walls around the top of the Sabika

plateau that were ultimately to enclose thirty-five acres. Like his father, Mohammed II contributed indirectly to the future Alhambra because his additional walls and towers later made it possible to build lavishly adorned palaces that were safe from attack.

By the second half of the thirteenth

The Alhambra is famous for the elaborate ornamentation of its interior decorations, as in this carefully worked window from the Hall of the Two Sisters (above left) and this inscription—which is incorporated into the overall geometric and floral design—from the Court of the Myrtles (above center).

century, the Alcazába had been remodeled into a substantial and well-equipped citadel. In the center was the large, triangular parade ground, now called the Plaza de Armas. Surrounding the entire fortress were sheer walls reinforced with strategically placed towers. Only eight of the original twenty-four towers remain today. Among these is the immense Torre de la Vela. Measuring over fifty feet square and more than eighty feet in height, it protected the citadel's original entrance—probably the only one at the time of Mohammed II. Today, the bell that sits on top of the tower is still used to regulate irrigation of the plains below. It also rings continually for thirty-six hours beginning the second day of every January in memory of

the act which marked the triumphant end of the Christian Reconquest of Spain.

Were it not for two of Mohammed II's successors, Yusuf I (1333–1354) and his son Mohammed V (1354–1391), the royal citadel of Granada would probably now be of but passing architectural interest. These two men were chiefly responsible for building the series of magnificent halls, chambers, tranquil courtyards, orchards, and gardens that are known today as the Alhambra.

Coming to the throne in 1333, the Nasrid king, Yusuf, vitalized all that he touched. During his reign, Muslim artists and craftsmen began to apply their abundant talents to the task of decorating the interior of the Alhambra. However, Yusuf did not take for granted the security of his palace-fortress. He entirely reinforced the Alcazába, rebuilt most of the royal residences of his predecessors, enlarged the ring of bulwarks that surrounded them, and further fortified the complex with additional towers. One of these was the Tower of the Ladies (Torre de las Damas), which has since been reconstructed. Even

though this tower was built principally for defensive purposes, it is—with its slender archway and many-windowed hall *(mirador)*—one of the Alhambra's most beautiful structures.

Near the end of his reign, Yusuf ordered a new gate to be built that would be a fitting entrance to the transformed Alhambra palace. This impressive portal—the Gate of Justice—is used today as the main entrance to the entire complex.

Perhaps the most spectacular architectural achievement that dates from Yusuf's time was the Court of the Myrtles (Patio de los Arrayanes). That the courtyard is primarily a pool of water may seem unusual to those from a Western culture, but water was an ultimate luxury to the Moors. As descendants of desert peoples, the Moors delighted in being able to incorporate water and vegetation into their architecture. In the Court of the Myrtles, the water lies motionless, reflecting delicate alabaster columns and weightless arcades of intricately carved plaster. The sides of the rectangular space are lined with lush myrtle hedges, and a narrow marble pavement borders the pool into which two circular fountains bubble softly.

At a right angle to this court is the second great court of the Alhambra, the Court of the Lions (Patio de los Leones), built under Mohammed V. This court is the most celebrated part of the Alhambra, with a quietly splashing alabaster fountain at its center. Twelve alabaster lions, probably dating back to the eleventh century, surround the fountain. Each lion is itself a small fountain, pouring water from its mouth into a narrow marble canal that also receives the waters of other smaller fountains in adjacent rooms via four narrow channels that form a cross.

Plants and flowers grow in between the narrow channels while slender alabaster columns, ribbed at the top, support an arcade of horseshoe arches of richly ornamented plaster, which encircles the courtyard. Colorful mosaic tiles cover the lower half of the walls. Not surprisingly, the Court of the Lions was reserved for the use of the royal family. Here, a king could stroll in complete solitude and find refreshment in the water, sunlight, gardens, and varied decorations that fill this outdoor sanctum.

Various halls and chambers were constructed by Yusuf and Mohammed V around these two principal courts. Though the Alhambra does not follow any formalized, overall ground plan, a definite sense of coherence is established through the grouping of rooms around courtyards. Thus, the waters that flow toward the Fountain of the Lions run northward from the Hall of the Abencerrajes, southward from the Hall of the Two Sisters, eastward from the Hall of the Mocárabes, and westward from the Hall of Justice. Another grouping centers on the Court of the Myrtles, which opens northward to the Hall of the Ambassadors. Between these two courts lie the baths, with their cool interiors of blue, green, yellow, and white mosaic tiles that were enjoyed by Yusuf and his successors. The Hall of the Ambassadors, which once contained the Nasrid throne, measures over thirty-six feet square and sixty feet high from the floor to the top of the dome. Ornamental

inscriptions from the Koran, which is the sacred book of the Islamic religion, abound throughout the hall. The largest room in the Alhambra and one of its most impressive, it was used as an official reception room for visiting dignitaries; its size was meant to impart a sense of the power and majesty of the Moorish state. Over this hall is a further display of power—a tower that must have reminded arriving ambassadors of Nasrid strength.

The Moorish architects imposed an order on the Alhambra—one as intricate

and complex as its ornamentation. The layout simultaneously suggests freedom and mystery, for the Alhambra is full of decorated archways—both single and in series—that might open into sunlit courtyards or perhaps look across colonnaded corridors into the retreating shadows of another arch or doorway. The many arched openings might also end abruptly or lead to some small, restricted space, such as the oratory where the praying Yusuf was assassinated by the frantic blade of a madman, or to a secluded *mirador* whose windows open out onto the

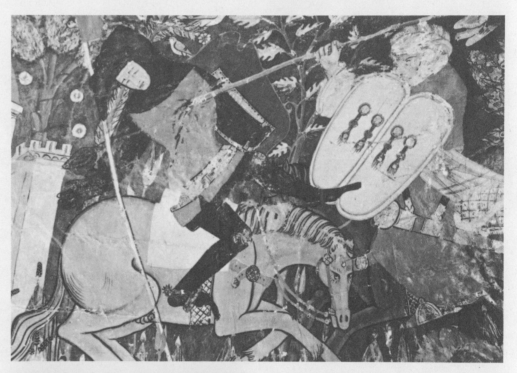

The portrayals of human figures in these two paintings from the Hall of Justice (also called the Hall of the Kings) are unusual decorations for the Alhambra. Forbidden subject matter to Muslim artists, these figures were probably painted by Mocárabes (who were Christians living in Muslim lands), perhaps under Muslim guidance.

fertile plains below. In this way, the Alhambra provides an endless series of changing views and perspectives. It is an architecture that resists simple or bold symmetric forms—either in overall plan or in ornamentation.

Since representational art was forbidden to the Muslims, their decorations were abstract: Geometric and floral patterns were created in plaster, stone, and ceramic tiles throughout the Alhambra. The ornamentation is elaborate and detailed, the patterns infinitely subdivided and refined.

By the beginning of the nineteenth century, wars, earthquakes, and human mistreatment had partially ruined the Alhambra. The illustrations on this page, which date from about 1835, capture a sense of this deterioration.

Left, the Gate of Justice built by Yusuf I in 1348.

Below, the Court of the Myrtles.

The decorations may seem to have a surface similarity, but the Moorish architects freely employed their imaginations to endlessly alter and embellish the designs handed down to them by hundreds of years of Islamic art.

Originally, these patterns were, most likely, brilliantly colored in blues, reds, and golds. The *azulejos* (colored tiles) were usually of green, yellow, blue, and white. The colors themselves normally remained constant from location to location, but their emphasis changed—gold might predominate in one pattern, red in another. Today, except for the tiles, the colors of the Alhambra have faded, and it is difficult to reconstruct exactly how color was used by the Moorish artists.

The Alhambra is renowned for one ornamental feature—the unusual stalactite configurations found in several of the halls. Here, intricate patterns of lacy, honeycombed stalactites, still mostly intact, hang from vaulted ceilings. The Hall of

the Two Sisters is the best example of this ingenious kind of ornamentation; the stalactite-covered cupola seems to be in the process of exploding, its particles surging outward and downward in fantastic, multicolored patterns.

The overall harmony of many elements—water, vegetation, landscape, buildings, and ornamentation—is an essential characteristic of the Alhambra's architecture. The integration is embodied in the design of the Court of the Lions, with its narrow water channels that connect the little fountains of the adjacent halls and porticoes with the large Fountain of the Lions in the center of the court.

A typical architectural device that exemplifies this quest for harmony is the *mirador*—a small, enclosed space with several arched openings that provide a variety of perspectives from which to enjoy the beauty of a secluded garden or the surrounding countryside. *Miradores* also modulate the harsh, Andalusian sunlight, illuminating some of the interior decorations while casting others into momentary oblivion. In many cases, especially in the towers, the *miradores* served a valuable defensive purpose, for there was a greater chance of spotting an enemy from multiple lookout stations.

Harmony of architecture and landscape is also found in the outlying gardens of the Generalife, which the kings and their favored guests used as a summer home. Here, in the still well-maintained Acequia Court, they could escape the pressures of office and be rejuvenated by the view of the plains below or by the sight and sound of the long, double row of fountains that runs the length of the garden. Members of the court could also stroll beneath the trees and among garden beds of fragrant herbs and flowers.

In one sense, the Alhambra has survived almost by chance, for the sovereigns of Granada never thought of building for eternity. Every Nasrid king wished to construct a palace that would satisfy his own taste and ceremonial requirements. This often involved destroying the work of his predecessors. In the case of Yusuf I and Mohammed V, this phenomenon turned out to be a boon to posterity, for their additions were magnificent.

Perhaps it is fortunate that their successors—who were struggling to keep the Spanish Christians at bay—had neither time nor money to spare for aesthetic pursuits; it would have been difficult for them to have improved upon the existing beauty of the Alhambra. Equally important, the Alhambra has survived at least in part because of the admiration with which its conquerors regarded the palace. One especially fervent admirer was Charles V, the Holy Roman Emperor and king of Spain who was so taken by the Alhambra that he commissioned the architect Pedro Machuca to build a palace within the Alhambra's walls. Begun in 1526, the palace was placed at the juncture between the Myrtle and Lion courts. In order to make room for it, an entire wing of the Alham-

Above, the base of a column on the east façade of the Palace of Charles V in the Alhambra. The stone carvings of the trophies of war represent recognizable military objects: armor, plumed helmet, crossbow, firearms, and, of course, the huge cannon that dominates the design. This ornamentation contrasts vividly with the abstract patterns of the Moorish architecture in the Alhambra.

Below, a portrait of Charles V of Hapsburg, the Holy Roman Emperor. Captivated by the beauty of the Moorish palace, Charles commissioned the architect Machuca to design a palace within the walls of the Alhambra. Of his many residences, Charles preferred Granada.

This Romantic engraving, called "Vermillion Towers," portrays the Alhambra as a forbidding castle from the legendary past, hiding dark secrets and bloody crimes. In fact, the Alhambra did have unsavory deeds associated with it, such as King Boabdil's slaughter of members of the Abencerrajes family—who had, according to various accounts, plotted against the king—in the chamber that now bears their name.

bra was destroyed. (A mosque was also destroyed in subsequent years to allow for a chapel on the east side of the palace.) The palace of Charles V remains unfinished to this day, yet it is still impressive with its large, round courtyard encircled by heavy, uniformly spaced columns.

Built in the style of the Italian Renaissance, the palace provides a dramatic contrast to the Islamic Alhambra. The design of Charles's bare palace is stern and solid, while that of the Alhambra is abstract and fluid. For example, tall, massive columns surround Charles's courtyard—which was used for great events like tournaments—while the slender and delicate columns of the Alhambra characteristically enclosed secluded gardens and pools.

Two different architectural traditions stand side by side at the Alhambra. But they reflect something that goes beyond architecture—a conflict of cultures. Islam eclipsed Christianity in southern Spain for nearly eight centuries, but its influence made Spain a far richer country. It is amazing that an "infidel" palace survived the Spanish Inquisition—so amazing that a myth was needed to explain the miracle. The Alhambra—as the story goes—was built by a necromancer who first sold his soul to the devil and then protected the palace with a magic spell.

Even so, the Alhambra has suffered many depredations over the years. In later centuries, explosions (set off by French troops in 1812), an earthquake in 1821, and human negligence resulted in a host of ailments: cracked walls and beams, broken windows, and crushed roofs and tiles. In rooms where Nasrid kings gave judgment and Charles V received ambassadors, gypsy children danced around the feet of stabled donkeys.

During and after the Napoleonic Wars, the Alhambra caught the imagination of a new, perhaps more romantically inclined, generation when it was "discovered" by the duke of Wellington, Washington Irving, and countless other less famous nineteenth-century tourists. Efforts were soon begun to restore the Alhambra, recapture some of its former glory, and protect a treasure that has been wrested once from the Moors and once from the ravages of time.

The Roman Forum

Italy

Preceding page, a general view of the Roman Forum as it appears today, looking eastward from the Capitoline Hill. In the right foreground are the columns of the Temple of Saturn, with the ruins of the Basilica Julia just beyond. Farther away stand the three remaining columns of the Temple of Castor and, to the left, part of the circular Temple of Vesta. The adjoining grassy rectangle was once occupied by the House of the Vestal Virgins—outlined by shattered sculptures of the virgins. The Sacred Way runs down the middle of the Forum.

Right, the Arch of Septimius Severus and the Column of Phocas—with capital—erected in A.D. 608, the last monument to be raised in the Forum.

Facing page, a section of the Arch of Septimius Severus, dedicated in A.D. 203 to the emperor and his two sons for their military victories in the East. This triumphal arch is covered with reliefs (detail above), many of which memorialize their conquests. The Temple of Castor, whose fluted columns stand beyond, was dedicated in 484 B.C. to honor Castor and Pollux—the mythical twins who heralded the decisive Roman victory at Lake Regillus.

Right, remains of the Basilica Aemilia, originally built in 179 B.C. It housed Rome's first water clock which, unlike the sundial, recorded the time during all weather conditions.

Saturn—who symbolized common prosperity—was a deity especially revered by the Romans. Founded in 497 B.C., the Temple of Saturn housed the treasury of Rome in underground vaults. The remains of the temple, shown here in three views, consist of eight granite columns of the portico. Nearby is the Rostra (lower left), the speakers' platform which clearly shows the holes used to attach the bronze battering prows from captured enemy ships.

Above, a partial view of the most sacred ground in Rome—the area dedicated to the service of Vesta. Plutarch tells us that the Temple of Vesta on the right was circular to imitate the shape of the universe, at the center of which was a fire known as Vesta. Accordingly, in the center of their temple, the vestal virgins guarded the sacred flame of state, never allowing it to die out. In the left foreground is the Aedicula Vesta, a small, outer shrine. Just beyond it is the Temple of Castor.

Left, the suovetaurilia—or joint sacrifice of sheep, pigs, and bulls—represented on the base of a column erected in the Forum to celebrate the tenth anniversary of the succession of emperors Constantius and Galerius.

Memories of the past are everywhere in the Forum, in the fragments (above) of a frieze from the Basilica Aemilia or in the base of an equestrian statue (right) erected in A.D. 353 in honor of the emperor Constantine

Left, the Ionic capital and entablature of the Temple of Saturn, which date from the fourth century A.D., when the Senate rebuilt the temple after it had been destroyed by fire.

Facing page, the columns of the Temple of Castor framed in a reconstructed arch of the Basilica Aemilia.

The oldest known Latin inscription is carved in the stele shown below. Written in archaic Latin, the inscription reads alternately from left to right and then from right to left. This ancient commemorative stone was found on the spot which, according to tradition, was the tomb of Romulus.

Following page, the setting sun seeming to cast an aura of timelessness on the Temple of Saturn.

The Roman Forum, Italy

Here, where the Forum now is, was once dense swamp: a ditch would drip with water that had flooded back from the river.

—Ovid

It must have been beyond the vision of the earliest settlers who beheld that unhealthy marsh to imagine it would become one of the world's greatest centers of civilization. Even Romulus, who according to legend founded the city in the eighth century B.C., could not have foreseen the transformation described above by Ovid, the Roman poet of the late first century B.C.

Writing several generations later, the brilliant satirist Juvenal complained of the deafening noise and confusion in the Roman Forum. Despite the great material progress of Roman civilization, he felt that it had deteriorated from a mere natural swamp into a moral one and that Rome had become a corrupt city where everything and everybody was up for sale.

Not everyone, of course, shared Juvenal's view of Rome. Other great writers, such as Horace, Virgil, and the historian Livy, presented the Roman character in a more balanced way, perceiving the special qualities that had enabled Rome to become a seminal world culture.

The ancients would hardly recognize the Roman Forum as it appears today. Where Cicero once inveighed against the

Right, a late seventeenth-century map of the ancient part of Rome. In the center of the map are some of the chief buildings and monuments of the Forum. When this map was made, the Forum was an untilled field known as the Campo Vaccino, or Cow Field.

conspirator Catiline and where Julius Caesar marched between the exultant cheers of the people and the jeers of the legionnaires (who were ordered to make fun of a victorious general at the moment of his triumph to restrain his ambitions), there is now a grassy field scattered with marble fragments—revealing traces of a once vital culture.

In the beginning, the Forum was nothing more than an open stretch of flat land that lay in the marshy valley between the Capitoline, Palatine, and Esquiline hills. Sometime during the sixth century B.C., an Etruscan king (whom Livy records as being Tarquin) channeled the many streams into one great drain, the Cloaca Maxima, which eventually emptied into the Tiber River.

The word *forum* may have derived from *foris* (out of doors) or perhaps from *forma*, implying an enclosed space designated for specific purposes. In any case, the reclaimed marsh provided a public place where farmers could put up booths on market days, sell their livestock, and meet their friends.

The subsequent growth of the city and the construction of temples, meeting halls, *tabernae* (shops), and monuments soon made the Forum the center of nearly every

aspect of Roman life—legal, political, religious, commercial, and social.

In the late fifth century B.C., the time of the early Republic, the Comitium was constructed. The historian Varro tells us that it was an open space where the Assemblies of Rome—representing the citizens—met with the Comitia Curiata. This was the group of senators housed in the small, plain building known as the Curia, which bordered the Comitium at the northwest end of the Forum.

The Curia—along with other buildings—had to be rebuilt after the sack of Rome in 390 B.C. by the Gauls. At that time, the Forum had run with the blood of senators who were butchered in their chairs when, despite warnings, they had stubbornly refused to leave the city to the Gallic invaders.

During republican times, the famed Rostra also came to play a major role in Forum life. It took its name from the *rostra*, which were bronze ships' prows used for ramming enemy vessels. In 338 B.C., the Romans captured the ships of Antium in an important naval battle against the Volsci. They brought home the ships and burned them but kept the *rostra* as trophies of their victory and used them to decorate the raised speakers' platform.

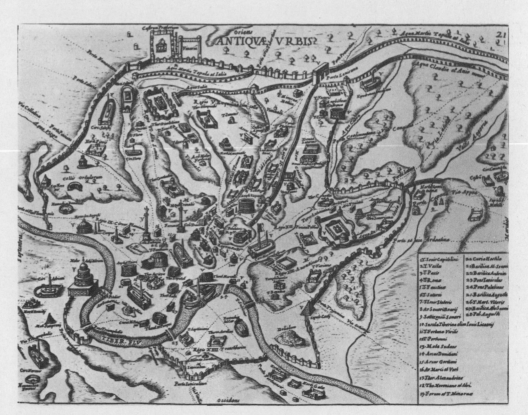

Cicero, the distinguished orator and statesman of the late Republic, accounted for his term as consul by saying: "I did nothing without the advice of the Senate, and the agreement of the people. I always defended the Senate in speaking from the Rostra, the people in speaking before the Senate." And it was with grotesque irony that Antony took revenge on Cicero, his political enemy: After having him murdered, Antony had his dismembered head and hands displayed from the Rostra, from which Cicero had so often addressed the people and defended the Republic.

During Cicero's time, and on into the period of imperial Rome, the Rostra was also used as a reviewing stand for ceremonial events such as triumphal processions, which would wind down the venerable Sacred Way that ran from the Capitoline Hill to the Arch of Titus at the eastern end of the Forum.

It is probably no accident that the Temple of Vesta, goddess of the hearth-fire, was centrally located in ancient Rome. Of the many Roman cults, the one dedicated to Vesta was the official state religion. The temple, the nearby grove, and the House of the Vestal Virgins occupied the ground the Romans held to be most sacred.

Plutarch tells us that the circular shape of the Temple of Vesta was designed to serve as an emblem of the universe, at the center of which was a fire known as Vesta. The six vestal virgins of Rome dedicated thirty or more years of their lives to chastity and to the service of Vesta by guarding the sacred flame—considered by the Romans to symbolize the state. These daughters of the state were, accordingly, highly privileged members of society; and it was cause for civic tragedy on the rare occasions when a vestal virgin was found guilty of sexual transgression. Her paramour was beaten with rods, but the disgraced woman was divested of her white robe, whipped, and carried through the streets on a bier in a grim procession while the citizens watched in tearful silence. She was transported outside the city limits to an underground crypt where a bed and meager provisions had been provided for her—it was considered a sacrilege to starve a former servant of a god and the state.

The idea of ancient Rome helped to inspire Napoleon's dream of an empire. It is somewhat of a historical irony that the Romans, whose imperial civilization had shaped the imagery of all post-Renaissance European art, would find themselves re-importing the trappings of that imperial civilization from the land of the Gauls—as in this illustration (left) of a Napoleonic statue of Liberty erected in the Forum in 1800.

Left, a 1773 view of the half-buried Forum. The Column of Phocas rises in the center.

Above, Cicero, the distinguished statesman and orator who was murdered by his political enemies. His head and hands were displayed on the Rostra, from which he had so often defended the Republic.

The crypt, with the fallen vestal virgin inside, was then sealed forever.

Other temples of the Forum were also an integral part of Roman life, such as the Temple of Castor constructed next to the spring of Juturna. Here, the deities Castor and Pollux were said to have stopped to water their battle-weary horses while bearing news of the imminent Roman victory at Lake Regillus in 496 B.C. In a speech, Cicero referred to the Temple of Castor as "that famous and noble monument, a temple placed where the eyes of the Roman people see it every day, where the Senate often meets, which is daily thronged by those who come to consult on the gravest issues."

The Temple of Saturn—one of the oldest and most revered of the Forum temples—was so intimately bound with the sanctity of the state that it contained the Aerarium, or the public treasury of Rome. Toward the end of the Republic in 49 B.C., when Julius Caesar occupied Rome, he boldly seized the Aerarium and removed, according to Pliny's figures, 15,000 bars of gold; 30,000 bars of silver; and 30,000,000 sesterces (a Roman coin).

The laws and regulations for constructing private houses were displayed on a bronze plaque behind the temple. Today, only eight granite columns of the portico—dating from the time of its reconstruction in the fourth century A.D.—remain of this monument honoring Saturn, who to the Romans symbolized common prosperity.

The Roman mint—housed nearby on the Capitoline Hill, the base of which marked the western end of the Forum—was contained within the Temple of Juno Moneta. During the Gallic sack of Rome in 390 B.C., the frantic honking and flapping noises of geese, which were the sacred creatures of the goddess Juno, awoke the drowsing Romans atop the Capitoline. This advance warning came just in time, for the invaders were already ascending

Above, a highly romanticized, nineteenth-century artist's rendition of rape and pillage in the Roman Forum and on the Capitoline Hill.

the hill. Juno became known to the Romans as Moneta, the "admonishing one." And so it happened that the Italian word *moneta* and the English word *money* derived from the Latin word for *warning*.

The Roman Forum, the architectural embodiment of the ideas and experiences of a rapidly expanding culture, evolved with that culture and became increasingly complex. During the second century B.C., the basilica began to appear as an architectural type and gradually became a standard feature of all the later forums, not only in Rome but also throughout the empire. The first of these in the Roman Forum was the Basilica Porcia, built in 184 B.C., followed five years later by the Basilica Aemilia, which was positioned behind the *tabernae* of the silversmiths on the northeast side of the Forum.

Though the word *basilica* is of Greek origin, the architectural concept is Roman. The republican basilica was characteristically a large, roofed hall, rectangular in shape, with either two or four colonnaded aisles flanking a central, raised nave. The basilica, as developed by the Romans, was later used as a model for many Christian churches, even though it did not serve a religious function in the Forum.

Space became increasingly critical as the city grew in population and wealth, and the basilica was ideally suited to accommodate a variety of activities in a single location. In fact, it came to be a kind of indoor forum, housing much of the political, legal, and financial business formerly performed in such diverse places as the temples, *tabernae*, the Curia, and the Comitium. This was especially true of the Basilica Julia, dedicated by Julius Caesar in 46 B.C., which was large enough to contain four legal tribunals as well as the many tables of the moneychangers.

Julius Caesar, who stands at the crossroads of republican and imperial Rome, began the series of alterations that permanently transformed the Roman Forum. He inaugurated the city's first urban renewal project and helped determine the final shape of the Forum. The placement of the Basilica Julia, the enlargement of the Curia, and the relocation of the Rostra to the extreme western end of the Forum at the base of the Capitoline were all changes that served to regularize the proportions of the Forum.

But Caesar also envisioned a second forum to the north of the old one. For the first time, a complex of monumental structures was planned outside the limits of the Forum proper—both as an expression of the power of a single individual identified with the state and in answer to the increasing need for greater space. Like Caesar, the emperors Augustus, Vespasian, Nerva, and Trajan each built his own forum, in a sustained series of urban building programs that reflected the ripening of the Roman Empire.

Eventually, the empire began to disintegrate. When it finally died, Rome's Forum died with it. Throughout the centuries, fires, wars, looting, earthquakes, and the spoilage of time reduced the Forum to ruins. The world seemed to turn its back on the square that had once been the center of one of history's most powerful empires. The stone that proudly marked the *umbilicus urbis Romae* (the navel of the city) lay buried, along with other ancient monuments beneath thirty to fifty feet of rubble. One could only glimpse the tops of the tallest monuments, most of which were added during imperial times—the Arch of Septimius Severus, the Arch of Titus, and the Column of Phocas, which was the last one to be erected in the Forum (A.D. 608).

Although the writings of the ancients had fueled the flame of the Renaissance, the vestiges of ancient Rome, once a living city, lay buried and forgotten beneath the rubble. Until the eighteenth century, the Forum had been inelegantly known as the Campo Vaccino, or the Cow Field, and had served as a cattle market. This certainly was not quite the vision of pastoral simplicity that Virgil had in mind when he created his epic the *Aeneid*, in which he imaginatively led Aeneas and his guide Evander over a still virginal Palatine Hill, from which "on all sides they saw cattle, where now is the Roman Forum."

Below, an overscaled vision of the Forum of Augustus by Giambattista Piranesi, the eighteenth-century Italian artist and architect who is famous for his imaginative engravings of ancient Roman monuments.

Heidelberg Castle

West Germany

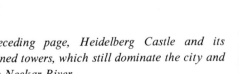

Preceding page, Heidelberg Castle and its ruined towers, which still dominate the city and the Neckar River.

Above left, the famed palace of the elector Otto Heinrich. It is flanked (left to right) by the roofless Apothecary and Clock towers. Above the entrance stands the Gate Tower (above right) ornamented with the so-called Giants of the Gate and the great clock. Right, the Broken Tower (Gesprengterturm) in the foreground and the Apothecary Tower beyond. Both of these towers overlook the beautiful, tree-filled moat. Left, the courtyard, seen here from the Friedrichsbau.

Below, the English Wing, which was built by the young elector Frederick V for his wife Elizabeth Stuart, the daughter of James I of England; and the great tower, the Dickerturm, which he transformed into a formal banquet hall. Both were destroyed by the French in the seventeenth century.

The palace of the elector Otto Ludwig V displays the coat of arms (left) of the elector and the date of construction (1524).

Facing page, the splendid wing built by Frederick IV (below), who was elector Palatine from 1592 to 1610. It stands between the Women's Wing and the Hall of Mirrors. The façade, which was strongly influenced by the façade of the palace of Otto Heinrich, is like a family tree. The niches between the windows contain statues of fifteen of Frederick IV's ancestors. Shown here (left to right) are Rupert III, who built another wing of the castle; Emperor Ludwig; and King Otto of Hungary.

RVPERTVS
REX ROM.
MCCCCX.

LVDOVICVS
IMPERAT
MCCCXIII.

OTTO REX
HVNGARI:
MCCCXII.

The wing of Otto Heinrich (above and below left), destroyed by lightning in 1764, is an undisputed masterpiece of German mannerist architecture. It was designed in 1556 by the elector himself, who came to reside in the castle when he was over fifty years old. The elaborate but delicate ornamentation forms a frame for the statues in their niches.

Facing page, the façade of the palace of Otto Heinrich, seen from the wing of the Hall of Mirrors. The focal point of the façade is the doorway, above which appears the coat of arms of the elector, surmounted by his portrait framed by a medallion. The entrance—with its solemn, triumphal arch—was dedicated to the glory of a dying princely lineage.

Parts of the castle have been patiently restored, including the gallery on the second floor of Frederick's wing (above left), with its finely ornamented ceiling. The pictures on the walls depict the ancestors of the elector, as do the statues opposite them. The collapse of an arch in the medieval chapel (above right) prompted Frederick to design and build a new palace, the Friedrichsbau (far right). Right, statue of Justice which was on the roof line of the Friedrichsbau. Far left, the famous barrel of 1750, which holds 58,000 gallons of wine, and (left) the small study used by Count Charles de Graimberg, an émigré noble who undertook the restoration of the castle in the nineteenth century.

Following page, a misty view of the castle in the early morning.

Heidelberg Castle, West Germany

High upon a wooded mountain, overlooking a small town and the Neckar River, stands the romantic, red sandstone castle of Heidelberg. Throughout its history, the castle has performed a double role, both as a fortress and as a home of the arts. Its austere, fortified walls and towers contrast harmoniously with the decoratively mannerist buildings within and the surrounding Italian gardens. Although the once vital castle now stands in ruins, it still retains a special beauty and bears vivid witness to centuries of German history and culture.

The original castle at Heidelberg was built toward the end of the twelfth century by the first count Palatine of the Rhine, Conrad von Hohenstaufen. Conrad, who was a brother of Emperor Frederick Barbarossa, first saw the medieval village of Heidelberg when he sought shelter at a monastery and was captivated by the beauty he saw around him. He obtained the land from its overlord, the bishop of Worms, and built a fortress on a bilberry-covered hill, from which the name Heidelberg was undoubtedly derived—for *heidelberg* means hill of the bilberries. Nothing remains of the original twelfth-century castle, but as befitting the home of a warrior-prince, it was probably a massive structure with thick walls and few windows. Legend has it that the first collection of German love lyrics was composed within its walls—an early German example of the courtly love poetry that had originated in Provence in the south of France.

Perhaps apocryphal, the story nevertheless points to the strong association of Heidelberg and the arts. By 1386, the third oldest and perhaps most famous of German universities was founded there as, a century later, was the celebrated Palatinate library, further establishing Heidelberg's pre-eminence as a center of art and culture. The court of the electors Palatine came to welcome the most influential German humanists—artists, writers, philosophers, and poets—within the medieval castle walls.

Otto Ludwig V of the Wittelsbach line grew up in this enlightened climate and became elector in 1508. He was responsible for the first important reconstruction of the castle since the fourteenth century, when it became the official residence of the electors Palatine. Ludwig enlarged the castle to its present size and strengthened its defenses by reinforcing the existing towers, which were provided with platforms for culverins and mortars, and opening arrow slits. More important, he built the Dickerturm, a stout tower whose walls in some places measured over twenty feet thick. Though in ruins, the tower is still imposing, as is the Gate Tower, with its bas-relief statues—the Giants of the Gate—and enormous clock. In addition to an arsenal and a deep moat, Ludwig added the elegant bell tower, with its circular base and polygonal upper stories.

In contrast to the medieval, warlike exterior of the castle, Ludwig transformed its interior into an elegant palace, famous for its frescoes, rich tapestries, and furnishings. To accommodate his court, which had become diverse and complex, Ludwig tore down the untidy jumble of modest dwellings around the castle and replaced them with residential and administrative wings. He built the guardhouse, a powder magazine, the vast kitchens with huge fireplaces (which can still be seen today), storehouses for grain and flour, and work-

Below, the town of Heidelberg and the castle, shown in an illustration dated 1620.

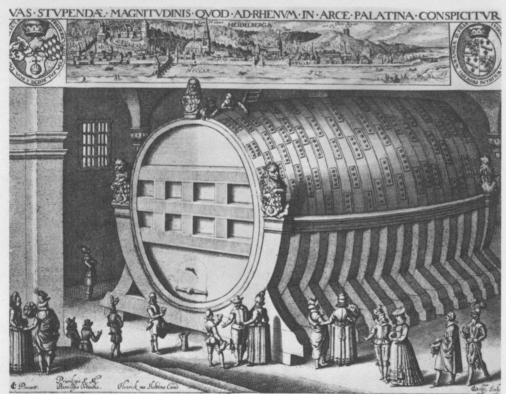

Left, the castle seen from the Hortus Palatinus, the splendid Italian garden commissioned by the elector Frederick V (above left) for his young English bride. Their son Rupert (above right), one of thirteen children, grew into the dashing prince who led the cavalry of Charles I during the English Civil War.

Below left, the first great barrel. Built in 1591, it had a capacity of almost 34,500 gallons of wine, which actually represented only a small portion of the wine received as tribute by the elector.

them in a way which imaginatively combined classical and Gothic styles.

Ludwig's building, with its pinnacled towers and steep roofs broken by pointed dormer windows, epitomized the severe grace of the Gothic. But it was an autumnal flowering—the Gothic world was in decline. In 1546, two years after Ludwig's death, his successor built the wing of the Hall of Mirrors. Mingling late-Gothic and Renaissance tastes, the Hall of Mirrors was an elegant ballroom, splendidly decorated with shining Venetian mirrors that contributed to an overall impression of airy lightness.

The Masterpiece of German Mannerism

With the flowering of the Renaissance, the thoughtful and cultured princes of the sixteenth century were no longer content to be mere patrons of the arts but often aspired to become artists themselves. One such artist-prince was Otto Heinrich, a passionate bibliophile, scholar, and collector of drawings and prints, who returned to the Palatinate in 1556 when he

shops for the smiths, armorers, tailors, and carpenters. Ludwig also constructed the so-called Women's Wing which, despite its name, housed the famous King's Hall. This served variously as a banquet hall, an armory for tournaments, and a workshop for court sculptors.

Another of the wings built by Ludwig now bears his name. A simple, late-Gothic building with a steep roof and slender pinnacles, it displays the coat of arms of the elector and the date of construction

(1524). But the work which most clearly exhibits the elector's humanistic spirit is the Brunnenhalle, or loggia of the well. High above the parapet of the well, five slender vaults meet to form a star. They rest on five granite columns, plundered from ancient Rome. According to legend, Charlemagne himself brought the pillars all the way from Magonza to Ingelheim, where they were used for his palace. Hearing of their beauty, Ludwig had them brought to Heidelberg, where he used was in his fifties, after having spent years abroad in foreign courts. Acting as his own architect, Heinrich designed and built his addition to the palace. He exploited to the full all the richness of the mannerist style, designing a façade in which architecture, ornamentation, and sculpture were carefully integrated to achieve a unified effect. Particularly notable is the series of statues of ancient gods, goddesses, muses, and virtues, masterfully carved by Alexander Colihn. Standing in niches between the windows, they celebrate the elector's cultured taste. The façade incorporates a doorway that bears the elector's portrait and coat of arms.

In the following decades, only one minor addition was made within the castle; a barrelhouse was built on the north wall, in which the wine given as tribute to the electors was stored. In 1591, a huge barrel which could hold almost 34,500 gallons was installed. In 1750, the elector Carl Theodore replaced this barrel with an even larger one, which could store more than 58,000 gallons.

Toward the end of the sixteenth century, part of the castle required substantial restoration. Not yet thirty, the elector Frederick IV seized this opportunity to build a residence in the castle that would reflect his educated sensibility. With the aid of his architect, a sculptor, and the court historian, Frederick soon laid plans for an elaborate mannerist façade. Not surprisingly, it was greatly influenced in both design and conception by Heinrich's monumental work. Begun in 1601, the magnificent façade of the Friedrichsbau took six years to complete. Set within special niches are fifteen statues of the Wittelsbach ancestors—and one of Frederick, one of the last of an ill-fated dying line. Among the majestic dynastic forebears represented are Charlemagne, Ludwig of Bavaria, and two royal—but distant—cousins: a king of Denmark and a king of Hungary.

Below the façade, Frederick also constructed a vast terrace, which not only overlooked the valley but also served as a stage for the continual spectacle of court activities and entertainments.

Frederick IV's son was only fourteen when he became elector Palatine. It had already been arranged that Frederick V should marry Elizabeth Stuart, daughter of James I of England. Surprisingly, the marriage proved to be exceptionally happy. In his desire to provide gracious surroundings for his English bride, Frederick further transformed what had begun as a severe, twelfth-century fortress into a fairy-tale castle.

For his English wife, Frederick built the English Wing, with a high, refined façade overlooking the town. He also increased the height of the Dickerturm and converted it into an enormous banquet hall, supported by a single central pillar. With great windows opening onto the surrounding green hills, this hall was used for all the most splendid court functions.

The festivities in honor of Frederick's English bride lasted for weeks, with dances, hunting parties, and theatrical performances. It is even said that Shakespeare himself, who would have been an old man at the time, played his last role as Prospero in *The Tempest* for the occasion.

The gloomy ramparts under the western tower were transformed into lovely gardens, named the Gardens of the Cannons in memory of their former military function. Elizabeth, dressed in white brocade and attended by her suite, entered the gardens through a baroque triumphal arch known as Elizabeth's Gate, which was purportedly built and carved in her honor from solid stone in a single night.

Frederick also laid out a huge Italian garden, the Hortus Palatinus, beyond the bare north and east ramparts. Its broad terraces were enlivened with fine statues of nymphs and goddesses, silvery fountains, and green foliage. In the same year that the garden was completed, Frederick—later dubbed the Winter King—left his verdant surroundings to accept the throne

Left, Count Tilly, who defeated Frederick V at the Battle of the White Hill outside Prague in 1620. This battle, one of the first of the Thirty Years' War, cost the elector both the throne of Bohemia and the Palatinate. The Gesprengterturm (below) is today known as the Broken Tower. The tower is a reminder of the savage wars that devastated Europe in the seventeenth century.

of Bohemia. His decision led him directly into the Thirty Years' War—with disastrous consequences for the Palatinate and the town of Heidelberg.

Destruction—and Restoration

When, after years of fighting, Frederick's son Carl Ludwig returned to Heidelberg, he found the castle despoiled and the beautiful gardens run wild. Carl Ludwig valiantly threw himself into the task of restoration, but the castle almost seemed to be condemned by its beauty. When Louis XIV's army invaded the Palatinate in 1688, the town of Heidelberg was on the blacklist of the French general Mélac.

The Palatine princess Elizabeth Charlotte, sister-in-law to the Sun King, pleaded in vain for the castle to be spared. On March 2, 1689, after a winter of bloodshed and suffering, the beautiful palaces of the electors Palatine were mined, covered with boiling pitch, and set

ablaze. The upper floors of the Women's Wing came crashing down; the sturdy Dickerturm was torn apart by explosions and fell in pieces into the burning town below. Still, much of the red sandstone structure did manage to withstand the fire—only to sustain further ravages five years later when, through the treachery of an officer, Heidelberg fell into the hands of the French for a second time.

Within a few years, the elector Johann Wilhelm began plans for rebuilding his devastated ancestral home, but he died before they were realized. Succeeding electors established themselves in the new baroque city of Mannheim, and the castle was almost totally abandoned. In 1764, lightning and fire destroyed the Otto-heinrichsbau and the once lustrous Hall of Mirrors, completing the devastation begun by the French.

During the nineteenth century, Heidelberg witnessed a renaissance of art and culture. The city came into its own again as the cradle of German Romanticism, while the castle itself was immortalized in

Above, Heidelberg Castle as it appeared before the most recent restorations. It was demolished twice by French armies, once in 1689 and again in 1693. In 1764, a fire caused by lightning completed the castle's ruin with the destruction of the Ottoheinrichsbau.

the poetry of Goethe, Longfellow, and Hölderlin, and in the paintings of Turner and Wallis. Toward the end of the century, the émigré French aristocrat and painter Charles de Graimberg fell under the spell of Heidelberg and resolved to restore the castle that had seen so much damage at the hands of his countrymen. Renting a room in the castle, Graimberg devoted the remainder of his life to studying the history of the castle, sketching its ruins, and raising money for its restoration. It is largely due to his efforts that the great broken castle above the Neckar River has retained its power to capture the imagination while regaining much of its original beauty.

St. Peter's

Vatican City

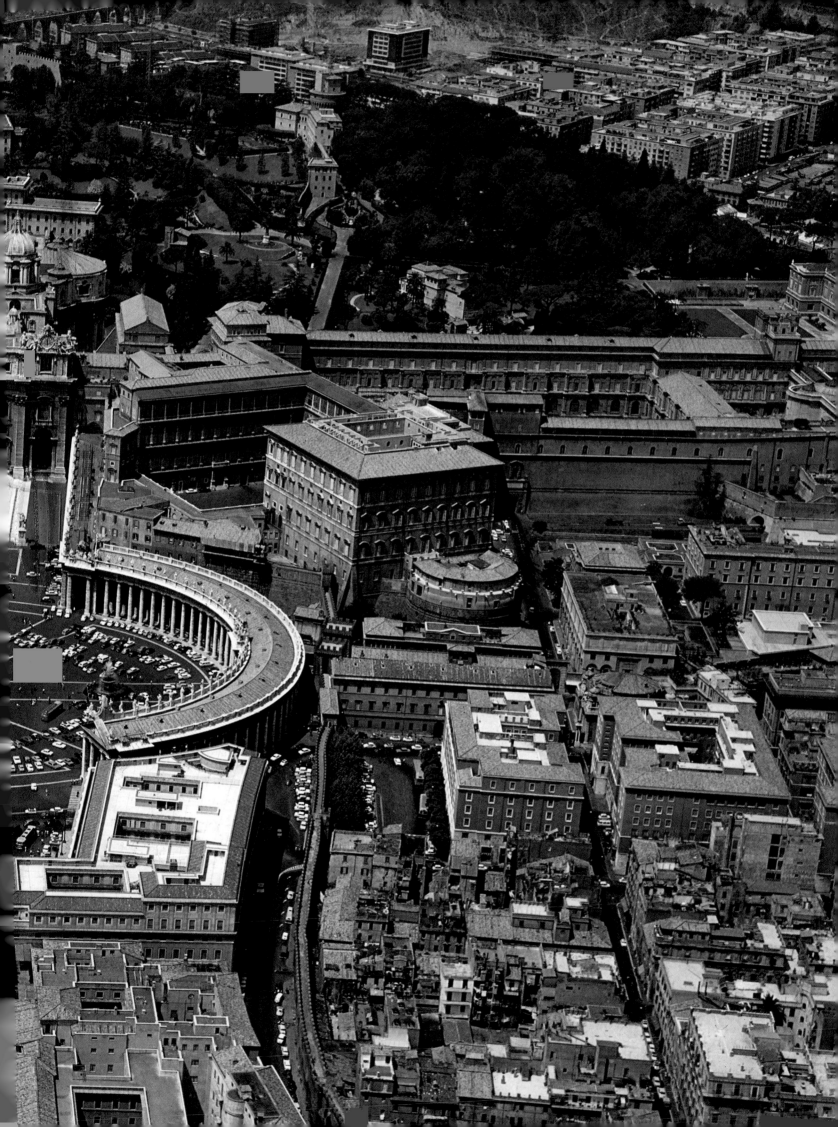

Preceding page, an aerial view of St. Peter's.

The "ecumenical embrace" of the colonnade and the aspiring thrust of the dome—these are the symbols of Catholic Rome, as the Colosseum is a symbol of pagan Rome. In 1694, the architect Carlo Fontana noticed with satisfaction that the piazza's colonnade exceeded that of the Colosseum by more than 1,600 feet.

The great colonnades encircling the piazza (above) were the work of Giovanni Lorenzo Bernini. Joined to the church by two diverging wings, they represent the encircling arms of the mother church.

Below, the façade by Carlo Maderno, completed in 1619. It has been criticized for obscuring the view of the dome. The two clocks date from the nineteenth century.

Above, the "open arms" of Bernini's piazza.
Bernini stated that architecture consists of an
interplay of proportions based on the human
figure. Here, the colonnade and the dome stand
in the same relation as the arms and head of a
man.

Far left, detail of the central entrance. Its bronze
doors were modeled for the previous basilica by
Antonio Averulino between 1433 and 1445.

Left, detail of the doors made by Giacomo
Manzu in the 1950s.

Right, the church as seen from the gardens of the
Vatican. This part of the building was designed
by Michelangelo.

The central aisles of the colonnades (this page) were reserved for carriages; the side aisles were for pedestrians. They were designed to provide shelter from rain or sun for the throngs of pilgrims who visited the basilica.

Facing page, a view of Michelangelo's dome.

Above, the vast interior of the basilica. Its magnificent proportions are deceptive: For example, the baldachino, or canopy, over the high altar is as high as a nine-story building.

Right, the famous canopy designed by Bernini with the help of Borromini. The beams from the portico of the Pantheon were melted down to provide the bronze for its construction. Its twisted columns echo the form of those of the baldachino that stood over St. Peter's tomb in the original Basilica of Constantine.

Left, two details of the Throne of St. Peter, also the work of Bernini. The throne is lit from behind by a window representing the Holy Spirit.

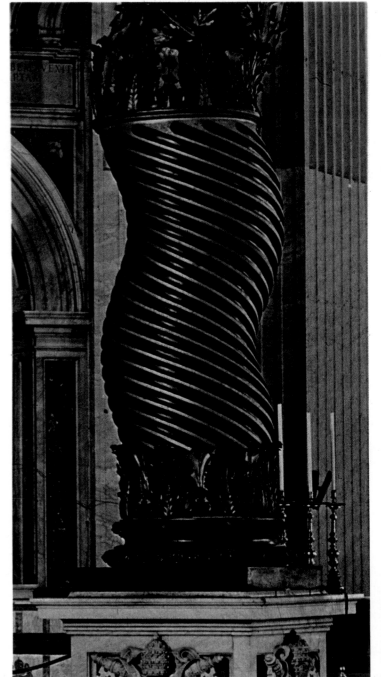

Details of Bernini's huge baldachino are shown here. Bernini was commissioned to make this canopy by Urban VIII, who became pope in 1623. His conception may have been influenced by smaller, processional canopies and by his experience as a designer of stage sets.

Facing page, the great vault of the central nave. This vault and those of the apse and transepts were intended by Michelangelo to be faced with travertine marble. However, in the eighteenth century, Luigi Vanvitelli covered the vaults with gilded stucco. The statues over the arches are by the school of Bernini.

Preceding page and left, the dome seen from inside the basilica. The dome of St. Peter's is about three feet smaller in diameter than the dome of the Pantheon but incomparably grander. At the beginning of the eighteenth century, a number of cracks appeared in the dome. The work of restoration was undertaken by Luigi Vanvitelli, who became the official Vatican architect in 1726.

On the frieze around the base of the dome (shown left and above) are the words used by Christ when he founded the Christian church: Tu es Petrus et super hanc petram aedificabo ecclesiam meam, et tibi dabo claves regni caelorum (*Thou art Peter, and upon this Rock I will build my Church, and I will give unto thee the keys of the Kingdom of Heaven*). The letters themselves are over six feet high. Below the frieze are circular mosaics that depict the Evangelists.

Above, view of the baldachino and apse.

Left, the nave as seen from the dome.

Four different views of the interior of St. Peter's are shown on this page. The Throne of St. Peter (left), designed by Bernini, stands in the apse. Below left, the shrine of the Pallia as seen from the "Confession" of St. Peter, an opening between the crypt and the nave, which Maderno placed in front of St. Peter's tomb. Above, one of the chapels in the choir. Below, the Grotte Nuove, excavated between 1534 and 1536 around the chapel of St. Peter, beneath the apse and transept of the basilica.

St. Peter's houses many papal tombs, decorated
with fine examples of Renaissance, baroque, and
neoclassical sculpture (facing page). The figure
of Charity (above left) forms part of the monument to Pope Innocent XII Pignatelli, which
was designed by Ferdinando Fuga and sculpted
by Valle. A second Charity (above right) was
designed by Bernini for the monument of Urban
VIII Barberini. A third Charity (below left)
stands at the left of the monument to Alexander
VII. This figure was also designed by Bernini
but executed by his pupil Mazzuoli. A figure
representing Religion (below right) watches over
the monument to Gregory XIII.

Above, St. Peter's Chair. Tradition claims that
the chair was actually used by the Apostle. It
dates from the late Roman Empire and is made
of wood inlaid with ivory (details at right).

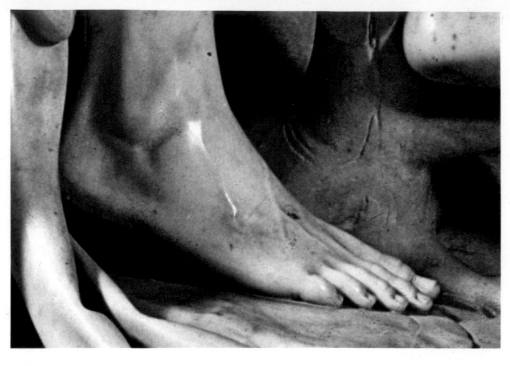

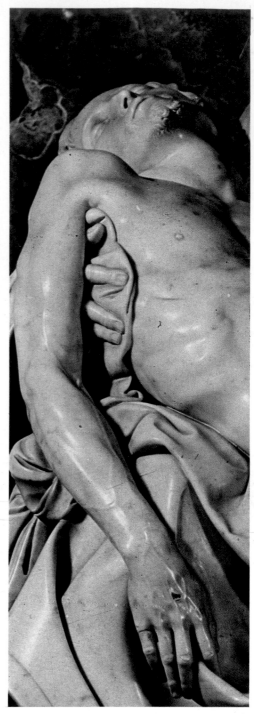

The Pietà (shown on these pages) by Michelangelo is the most famous work of art in St. Peter's. One of the artist's early works, it was sculpted between 1498 and 1500 for the French ambassador to the Holy See. It originally stood in the old St. Peter's but in 1535 was moved to the Capella della Febbre in the new basilica. For this reason, it is sometimes known as the Madonna della Febbre. Today, the Pietà stands in the Cappella del Crocifisso. Having been attacked by a madman with a hammer a few years ago, it is now sheltered behind a sheet of bulletproof glass.

Following page, details of the statuary of St. Peter's—human expression translated into bronze and stone.

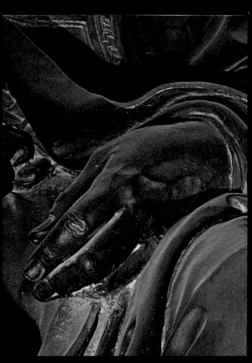

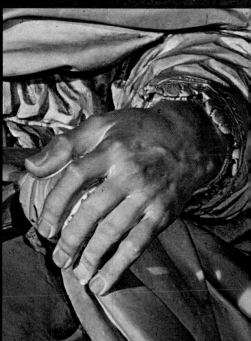

St. Peter's, Vatican City

The Basilica of St. Peter's in Rome is one of the most magnificent triumphs of the Renaissance. Housing the tomb of the leader of the Apostles, it is the center of the Catholic faith and its most venerated shrine, attracting countless pilgrims every year. Though the story behind the construction of this most holy of Catholic churches may be tinged with more than the usual measure of administrative and economic complications—including recurrent bureaucratic quarrels and personal squabbles—St. Peter's reflects the contributions of such illustrious architects and sculptors as Bramante, Michelangelo, Raphael, and Bernini.

The original Basilica of St. Peter's had been built in the fourth century by the emperor Constantine above the tomb of the Apostle and near the site of his martyrdom. By the middle of the fifteenth century, severe cracks were appearing in the old structure, which threatened to collapse. However, restoration work did not really get under way until after the election of Pope Julius II in 1503. A powerful ecclesiastical politician of noble birth, as well as a sworn enemy of the Borgias, Julius had an insatiable passion for building, and he immediately commissioned the distinguished architect Donato Bramante to remodel the Vatican palaces.

In undertaking another project—the renovation of St. Peter's—Julius was probably thinking more of preparing a place for his own monumental tomb than of

Facing page, Michelangelo's dome as seen from the papal gardens.

Below, the original St. Peter's as seen by Hartmann Schedel in 1493. Built in the fourth century by the emperor Constantine, it was the center of Christianity for over a thousand years.

Left, Pope Julius II of the della Rovere family who commissioned Bramante to design the new Basilica of St. Peter's.

Center, Donato Bramante, the first architect of St. Peter's. His work laid the foundations for all subsequent designs.

Right, Antonio da Sangallo the Younger, one of Bramante's successors. Almost nothing remains of his work on the great basilica.

The idea of a completely symmetric church—one symmetric about a single central point—had wide appeal in the sixteenth century.

Left, a rough sketch for a domed church by Antonio de Pellegrino.

Below left, an anonymous drawing with notes on how to build a dome. Below right, a sketch by Antonio da Sangallo the Younger.

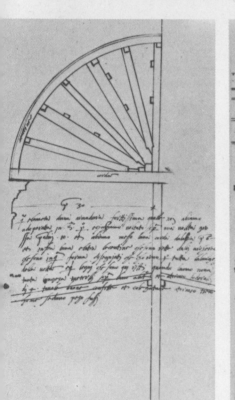

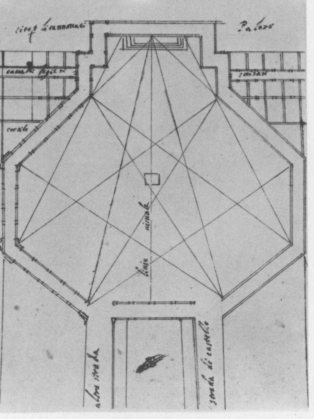

restoring the site of the tomb of the Apostle. Upon the recommendation of his artistic adviser, Giuliano da Sangallo, Julius engaged a promising young Florentine sculptor to design and build a splendid tomb for him in St. Peter's. The sculptor's name was Michelangelo Buonarroti.

Monumentally egotistical and temperamental, Michelangelo tended to ignore all opinions except his own. He designed a tomb so large and grand that it was generally considered to be out of proportion with the ancient basilica in which it was to be built. Nevertheless, Michelangelo left for Carrara to select the marble for its construction. During his absence, Pope Julius became convinced that St. Peter's was crumbling and dangerous; to be worthy of housing his sepulcher, it would have to be rebuilt completely. His decision was greatly influenced by Bramante, who inspired the pope with many ideas for a new basilica. It was eventually Bramante's design which was chosen over two others submitted for the project by Giuliano da Sangallo and Fra Giocondo da Verona.

When Michelangelo returned to Rome, he found that Pope Julius was totally preoccupied with Bramante's plans for the new basilica and that his own project had been shelved. He returned to Florence in disgust. His sepulcher was never built, but forty years later he was recalled to Rome to make an even greater contribution to the new basilica.

The original basilica built by Constantine was one of the largest and most venerable churches in Christendom. It had a nave and two pairs of aisles, separated by long colonnades. Before it stood the renowned "Paradise," an enclosed court with

Below, a study by Bramante for the design of St. Peter's. Bramante's design for a basilica with four great bell towers takes the form of a Greek cross, having similar, smaller crosses flanking the intersections of the nave and transept.

Right, Antonio da Sangallo the Younger's design for St. Peter's, which was ferociously attacked by Michelangelo. Sangallo retained the four central pillars, which had already been built by Bramante, but absorbed them into a design in the form of a Latin cross, which was noticeably less compact than Bramante's plan.

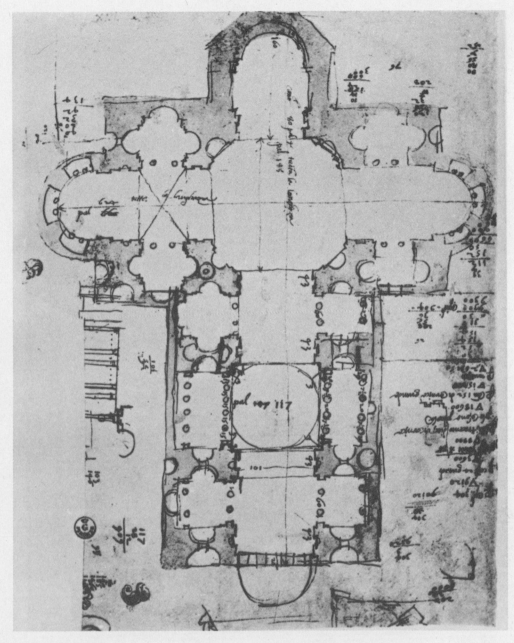

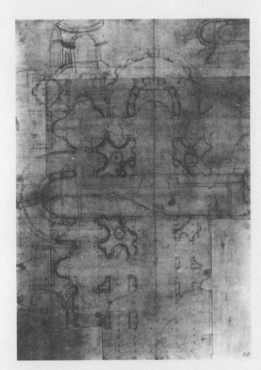

fountains. The basilica contained the tombs of many renowned popes and European kings and emperors as well as ancient paintings and beautiful mosaics. In A.D. 800, Charlemagne had been crowned at the basilica's high altar.

Within a few months, Bramante had demolished everything around the ancient altar. The people of Rome were shocked. On the old statue of Pasquino, where the Romans liked to hang their anonymous protests, Bramante was dubbed *Donato Bramante, Mastro Ruinante* (Bramante, the architect of ruins).

If Bramante did not show respect for Constantine's basilica, he at least had a remarkably bold and majestic plan for its successor. He had designed a church with a dome on the scale of that of the Pantheon, the greatest dome to have survived from antiquity. The new basilica was to be in the form of a Greek cross, each of whose four equal arms would be a nave. The dome of the basilica was to rise from the intersection of these naves. The Greek-cross motif was to be repeated in smaller domed spaces that would lie adjacent to the intersections of the naves. Great bell towers at the corners would complete the scheme. The overall design was based on a popular contemporary concept in church architecture: The dome, supported by four equal arms, was considered a symbolic representation of the universe, with the heavens suspended high above the four corners of the earth.

On April 18, 1506, when the first stone of the new basilica was laid, Bramante grandly stated another concept behind his design: "I will build the dome of the Pantheon upon the Basilica of Constantine." Pagan Rome and the vestiges of the old Christian Roman Empire were thus to be united symbolically and reborn.

Of course, the new basilica was meant to be above all a concrete symbol of the unity of the Roman Catholic Church. But, ironically, its construction contributed to the most decisive rebellion ever launched against the authority of the Church—the Protestant Reformation, a rebellion which

Signed sketches of designs for St. Peter's by Baldassare Peruzzi (top and left) and Antonio da Sangallo (center) are shown here. Although these architects were in charge of the reconstruction for many years, their contributions were minor and were discarded by Michelangelo.

was to divide the Church permanently. In 1517, Pope Leo announced a great sale of indulgences throughout Europe to finance the ongoing construction of the new basilica. Although the sale of indulgences was the traditional method of raising money for the Church, there was already a growing discontent with this medieval practice of spiritual exploitation. The extraordinary expense of rebuilding St. Peter's became one of the principal grievances upon which Martin Luther based his campaign

of secession from the Church of Rome. About a decade later, when the Lutheran mercenaries of Emperor Charles V sacked the Eternal City, the soldiers were to use the basilica as a stable for their horses—an obvious gesture of desecration.

Meanwhile, the task of reconstruction passed through the hands of a number of architects in rapid succession. Bramante died in 1514, and Pope Leo commissioned his rivals, Giuliano da Sangallo and Fra Giocondo, to continue his work. They were supervised, however, by the painter Raphael, who was considered by the Romans to be their finest living artist.

Only the four great piers of Bramante's basilica had actually been built. Raphael used these as the starting point for a radically different design, based on the shape of the familiar Latin cross of Christ's crucifixion, arranged with side aisles—almost the width of the nave—which were separated by rows of pillars. However, very little of Raphael's design was realized.

On his death in 1520, a new chief architect was chosen—Baldassare Peruzzi of Siena, the celebrated architect of the Farnesina, one of the most splendid villas on the edge of Rome. Peruzzi, who intended to return to the Greek-cross plan, was in charge of construction throughout the next sixteen years, but little of his design was carried out. Lack of money and his stormy relationship with his ambitious assistant, Antonio da Sangallo the Younger, impeded his progress. This Sangallo was the nephew of Guiliano da Sangallo, Pope Julius's adviser, and he made use of his uncle's good standing with the papacy. Eventually, Sangallo managed to take over full responsibility for the building project, and he redesigned the basilica, which was to be built once again in the Latin-cross form.

Michelangelo, for one, loudly censured Sangallo's design. He called it "blind" and "Gothic," which to him meant barbaric—architecture more suited to a den of thieves, an alehouse, or a brothel than to a church. In 1547, Michelangelo got his chance to improve upon it, when he was appointed overseer of building operations by Pope Paul III. Despite his previous

Above, a portrait of Michelangelo by Daniele da Volterra. Above center, Paul III Farnese, the pope who in 1547 commissioned Michelangelo to direct the building of St. Peter's. Above right, Paul V Borghese, the pope for whom Maderno added the nave and façade of the basilica.

Below, a working sketch of the interior showing Bernini's baldachino and Maderno's "Confession" of St. Peter.

harsh criticism of Sangallo, Michelangelo initially protested that he was a sculptor and not an architect. He finally accepted the appointment but refused to regularly visit the site, sending his assistants instead.

In spite of his old age and reputed inflexibility as a master builder, Michelangelo gave the church its most distinctive feature by returning to the original conception of Bramante. However, he modified Bramante's idea of a dome supported by a Greek-cross structure, simplifying and enlarging it, so that the church essentially became a huge platform for the gigantic dome. Michelangelo also chose not to model this dome after that of the Pantheon but rather after the great dome built by Brunelleschi for the Cathedral of Florence, which was said to be large enough to embrace "all the peoples of Christendom."

However, the dome of St. Peter's, known throughout the world as the masterpiece of Michelangelo, was not in fact erected by him. After the death of the master, it was completed by Giacomo della Porta and Domenico Fontana, with only slight modifications of Michelangelo's original design. Its shape was heightened during construction to more closely resemble its Florentine model. The plan of the church, however, turned out to be quite different from Michelangelo's conception.

If Michelangelo gave St. Peter's its dome and most renowned symbol, it was

Giovanni Lorenzo Bernini who made the interior and the enormous forecourt what they are today. Bernini took over supervision of the construction of St. Peter's in 1629, sixty-five years after the death of Michelangelo. The interim years had not been idle ones. After the dome was completed in 1590, the main structure was finished by Carlo Maderno under Pope Paul V in 1614. The completed basilica was in the form of a Latin cross, with a great entrance portico and a huge nave flanked by two side aisles and many chapels. Its transepts and apse were of equal sizes, having

Above left and left, study of a church on a central plan. St. Peter's is the finest example of this recurrent design in Renaissance architecture.

Below, two projects for the façade of the church. The first is of the school of Sangallo and was probably executed around 1505. The second, possibly by Bernardo della Volpia, has much in common with the façade which was finally designed and built by Maderno.

Facing page, illustrations by Maarten van Heemskerck showing the work on St. Peter's in about 1520, soon after Bramante's death. By starting in the center with the foundations for the dome, Bramante forced all his successors to respect the nucleus of his design.

been fashioned from three of the naves of the original Greek-cross scheme. The façade of the new church was also the work of Maderno. Its huge, half-round pilasters echoed, but did not copy, the existing external ornamental scheme conceived by Michelangelo.

Bernini's most notable contributions to the interior were the enormous, gilt bronze canopy over the high altar; the Throne of St. Peter in the apse; and the design and scale of the many statues and decorations which have the effect of scaling down the colossal proportions of the interior. However, Bernini is probably most celebrated for his great piazza in front of St. Peter's, with its obelisk and fountains. This work was commissioned by Alexander VII and executed between 1655 and 1667.

Not all of Bernini's projects received such approval. The new pope, Innocent XI, denied him funds to complete the colonnades of the piazza. Moreover, Bernini was held responsible for cracks in the main pillars of the church as well as those in Maderno's façade, where the architect had tried to add two bell towers. The pope even insisted that he clothe the statue of a woman representing Truth—which he found "too naked."

interno della Collonada di S. Pietro   Carlo Roos Wartembroghese
                                                            i Roma 1816.

Above, a view of Bernini's colonnade by an unknown (probably German) artist of the early nineteenth century. The central passageway in the ring of columns was designed by Bernini for horse-drawn carriages.

Understandably, the new basilica was not very popular with the citizens of Rome, who were subjected to crushing taxation in order to finance its construction. Among the comments left at the statue of Pasquino was the epitaph for the monument of Pope Urban: *Orbem bellis, Urbem gabellis implevit* (He filled the world with wars and the city with taxes). The Church contended that the construction was of great social value, since it provided sorely needed employment. However, the wages left much to be desired, and the workmen on the site voiced their

protests with chants and placards expressing their need for bread, not obelisks and fountains.

Despite all the obstacles, St. Peter's today is probably unmatched in its historic and artistic richness. The heart of Catholic Christendom for two thousand years, it is the site of some of the world's most precious treasures. Michelangelo was not able to build his great tomb for Julius II here, but he did leave his miraculous Pietà. And here too are Bernini's altar canopy—fashioned out of bronze removed from the Pantheon—and Throne of St. Peter, a reliquary for a Roman chair the Apostle is purported to have used. Together, they dominate the interior of the basilica.

In 1929, Pope Pius XI signed the Lateran Treaty which renounced the Church's claim to any temporal sovereignty outside the Vatican, so that St. Peter's, once the heart of a state which controlled much of

Italy, now became but the enormous centerpiece of a tiny sovereign city. In celebration—more of his own power than of the event—Mussolini built the Via della Conciliazione leading up to the basilica, thus opening up an unobstructed view of Michelangelo's dome and, at the same time, radically lessening the sense of wonder and surprise previously experienced as one had suddenly emerged from the surrounding web of narrow streets into full sight of the largest and greatest of Renaissance monuments.

Temple of Amon

Egypt

Preceding page, the "holy city" of Karnak. Its two main roads—the processional ways of the gods—are lined with gateways, rows of sphinxes, temples, obelisks, imposing colonnaded hypostyle halls, and enormous portals (pylons). The lake, whose calm waters have reflected the monument for more than three thousand years, played an indispensable role in religious ceremonies at Karnak.

Facing page, two views of the Hypostyle Hall. Begun by Sethos I of the Nineteenth Dynasty, it was completed by his son Rameses II, from whom many believe the biblical Hebrews won their freedom under the leadership of Moses.

Above, a wall and mighty papyrus-shaped column covered with reliefs portraying the military achievements of the Nineteenth Dynasty.

Above right, the great gate of Ptolemy III on the southern side of the outer walls of the temple, on the road from Karnak to Luxor.

Below right, the "Vestibule of Bubastis," built by the pharaohs of the Twenty-second Dynasty (ca. 950–730 B.C.), who originally came from Bubastis on the Nile Delta.

Above left, statue of Rameses II. The buildings of Rameses II included dozens of statues of the pharaoh in many sizes, from the small effigies between the paws of the sphinxes (on the processional way) to the monumental colossi in which he appears both with and without the red and white "double crown" of Upper and Lower Egypt.

Left, the processional temple of Rameses III (1182–1151 B.C.). Its portico is supported by huge, mummylike statues of the pharaoh.

Above and facing page, statues representing Rameses II. The figure at his knees represents his wife.

Several views of the processional temple of Sesostris I, pharaoh of the Twelfth Dynasty, are shown here. Built of limestone and lavishly ornamented, the temple's fragments were extracted from a later pylon and reassembled by archaeologists. Its reliefs are among the most intriguingly detailed in Karnak. A miniature version of the central shrine of the temple, it was a stopping place for the acolytes who carried the god's processional boat on their shoulders.

Above, details of the vast columns of Rameses' Hypostyle Hall. All the columns—except the taller, central ones—are shaped like bundles of papyrus. The closed corolla of the papyrus bundles forming the capitals symbolizes the power of fecundity of the god of Amon.

Below, the avenue of the sphinxes erected by Rameses II, leading to the mighty but unfinished first pylon built by Nectanebes I in the Thirteenth Dynasty.

Facing page, the ram-headed sphinxes in the avenue leading to the great shrine.

Following page, the banquet chamber of Tuthmosis III (1504–1450 B.C.).

Temple of Amon, Egypt

The energetic princes who governed the ancient Egyptian city of Thebes over three thousand years ago were political rivals of the pharaohs who ruled from Heracleopolis in the north. The princes of Thebes eventually emerged as supreme sovereigns when they united the provinces of Upper and Lower Egypt under the Eleventh Dynasty (ca. 2130–1990 B.C.). This was the beginning of an era of the large-scale religious monuments and the origin of the great temple complex, whose ruins stand today at Karnak on the banks of the Nile in central Egypt—the site of the vanished city of Thebes.

At the height of its power, Karnak was a gargantuan sandstone maze of massive gates, ranks of columns, and vast rectangular halls, which were carved with splendid reliefs attesting to the glory of the gods and pharaohs. Most of the temple walls were patterned in bright blues, greens, and luminous reds. Other walls, in striking contrast, were stark white. Over the centuries, the colors have faded, and the gold and precious stones which once embellished the innermost sanctuaries have been plundered.

The Rise of the Great Amon-Re

Up to the Eleventh Dynasty (which was the beginning of the Middle Kingdom), Amon, the god of the princes of Thebes, had been a mere household god, little more than a totem. However, as the protecting deity of the reigning dynasty, he gained stature. And as he grew in importance, the little brick and stone temple which had been built as his sanctuary on the east bank of the Nile became the nucleus of a series of enlargements. The ancient name of the temple complex was Ipet-isut, or Epte-sowe (Chosen of Places). Every Egyptian dynasty for the next two thousand years was to leave its lavish mark of devotion on the temple of the great Amon-Re.

During the Twelfth Dynasty (ca. 1990–1785 B.C.), a group of Asian wanderers called the Hyksos (shepherd kings) invaded and dominated all of Egypt except Thebes. The princes and priests of Thebes were the leaders in a struggle for reconquest which lasted for generations. At that time, the Theban god Amon became the symbol of Egyptian resistance to foreign invasion. The son of the founder of the Twelfth Dynasty, Sesostris I, built a white limestone chapel beside the original temple to celebrate his jubilee—the anniversary of his marriage to power. As with many buildings at Karnak, the chapel was dismantled by a subsequent king who used the materials to build his own structures and to reinforce his ascendancy over previous rulers. However, modern archaeologists have been able to reconstruct the chapel built by Sesostris I by piecing

Below, Karnak in an early archaeological map, drawn by a nineteenth-century French scholar. The map shows the Temple of Amon and the temple of his wife Mut joined by a processional avenue.

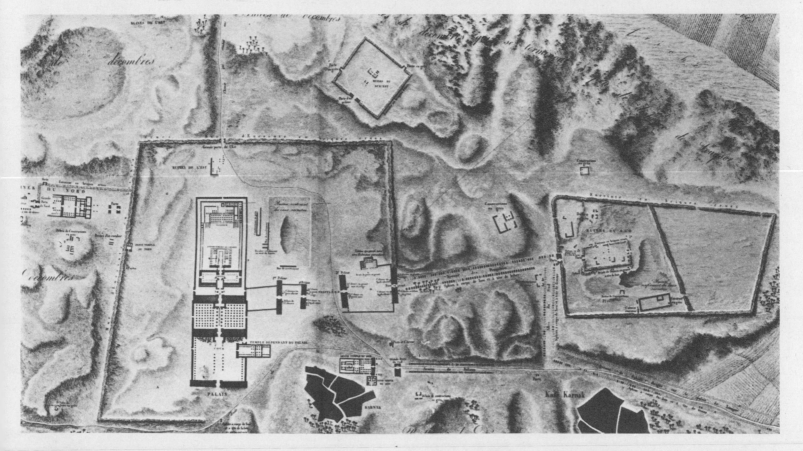

Above, a bas-relief of a carpenter's shop, with men at work cutting and squaring massive beams. At the temple site, there were a large number of these workshops.

Right, a relief showing the fastidious morning toilette of an Egyptian princess.

Far right, Senenmut, architect-scribe and favorite of Queen Hatshepsut. He supervised Hatshepsut's improvements and additions to the Temple of Amon at Karnak.

Above, Queen Tiy, wife of Amenhotep III. This head—carved in yew, painted in gold, and set with jewels—is a wonderful example of the art of the New Kingdom, the era in which the most famous structures of Karnak were built.

together fragments found within later structures at Karnak.

Around 1560 B.C., the Theban kings finally succeeded in driving back the Hyksos. The reconquest of Egypt signaled the beginning of the Eighteenth Dynasty and the New Kingdom, which was an era of great prosperity for Thebes. After Amon's warrior sons gained Egypt's sovereignty, the mythology surrounding Amon expanded as he grew to be the majestic god of a mighty nation. In time, he became known as the great Amon-Re, taking on the attributes of the ancient sun god Ra. He acquired a wife, the goddess Mut, who bore him a son—the moon god Khons.

Elaborate ritual processions were a regular part of the ceremonial worship. The two grand processional ways, one toward the river and one leading south toward the city and the Temple of Mut, eventually formed the axes of the enormous complex of Karnak. On either side of these main axes were monuments to the power and wealth of the pharaohs: processional temples, monumental gateways, and avenues of sphinxes leading to the sanctuary of Amon-Re.

It was the pharaohs of the Eighteenth and Nineteenth dynasties who built the largest and grandest monuments and temples to Amon-Re. During the Eighteenth Dynasty (1567–1320 B.C.), the temple was encased within a huge sandstone wall. A great gate on the western side of the temple was flanked by two massive towers. The gateway was painted in vivid colors and finished with bronze from Asia and gold from Sinai. Tall flagpoles hewed from the precious cedar of Lebanon and tipped with gold stood on each side of the gate, their long pennants wafted by the desert winds.

Tuthmosis I added a second ornate gateway outside the walls, mounted by two gigantic obelisks of red granite. A large reception room, with tall columns shaped like bundles of papyrus, was built between the two gateways. This structure was the most striking feature of the ancient complex with its so-called pylons, or massive gateways, and pillared hypostyle chambers. Ten pylons are still standing today in the ruins of the temple.

Tuthmosis' buildings were greatly altered by his daughter, Queen Hatshepsut. Hatshepsut married her half brother,

Tuthmosis II, according to the custom of the Egyptian pharaohs. However, the ambitious Hatshepsut became more than an honored consort. After her husband's death, she herself ruled Egypt as coregent with her husband's son, her nephew—Tuthmosis III.

A skillful ruler and administrator, Hatshepsut expanded the eastern side of Amon's temple to reflect her own power as pharaoh. She built another pylon along the processional way to the Temple of Mut and erected two obelisks at the rear of the temple. Demolishing the columned room between the two pylons of Tuthmosis I, she erected in its place two more obelisks, one of which still stands today and is the tallest in Egypt. Inside the shrine, she built a "sanctuary of the boat" for the ritual vessel in which—borne on the shoulders of the priests—Amon-Re was believed to have made his annual ceremonial visit to his wife Mut and his son Khons in their respective temples.

After Hatshepsut died, a violent reaction broke out against her. Feeling that Hatshepsut had overstepped her bounds as a woman (and that he had been overshadowed), Tuthmosis III had her name stricken from all monuments. Her sanctuary of the boat, scarcely finished, was demolished. In its place, Tuthmosis III built another chapel known as the Red Chapel because it was constructed in solid red granite.

Tuthmosis added another pylon and another hall, known as the Hall of Documents. He straddled the processional way, which Hatshepsut had built toward the city, with yet another pylon. Finally, he added many inscriptions chronicling his victories in foreign campaigns and endowed the sanctuary with an immense Festival Hall, flanked by another smaller room. The walls of this latter room, known today as Tuthmosis' Botanical Garden, were carved with a pictorial catalogue of the flora and fauna he had observed in his travels between the deserts of the Sudan and the cold waters of the Euphrates. A small temple dedicated to the god Ptah (patron of craftsmen whose cult centered in Memphis and flourished around 1320–

Left, a French scholar studying excavated artifacts. Napoleon returned from his Egyptian campaign with many treasures of antiquity. These treasures were first classified and arranged by a team of French archaeologists headed by Baron Dominique Vivant Denon.

Below, two sectional views through one of the little processional temples on the avenue to the temple. The walls and columns of these smaller structures are covered with fine reliefs which relate tales of the powerful Amon and his devotees.

1200 B.C.), a few obelisks, and a new enclosing wall completed his additions.

A successor to Tuthmosis III, Amenhotep III (ca. 1415–1380 B.C.), disassembled a number of temples to supply materials for his own monuments. (Purportedly, he combined a mania for building with a miserly streak.) In honor of Amon, he added another grandiose

pylon, from which a colonnaded avenue led to the entrance of the temple. He also built a series of temples dedicated to the lesser gods who had been neglected in favor of Amon-Re. His fanatical son actually attempted to completely replace the cult of Amon-Re with the worship of the sun god Aton. Amenhotep IV (ca. 1380–1360 B.C.) changed his name from "Amon

The huge pylons (left) and the ruins of the great Hypostyle Hall (below) as they must have appeared to the first modern Europeans to visit the temple.

is Satisfied" to Akhenaton, "It Pleases Aton," and abandoned Thebes, after having defaced the temples and monuments of Amon. However, after Akhenaton's death, his son-in-law Tutakhamen began to restore Karnak and revitalize the cult of the god Amon-Re.

The pharaohs of the Nineteenth Dynasty (1320–1200 B.C.) came from a family of self-made men—soldiers who won the trust of the previous pharaohs and eventually inherited the powers of the ancient line. As pharaohs, they continued to be great military leaders. They were also responsible for the Hypostyle Hall, one of the most inspiring structures at Karnak. Begun by Sethos I, the hall was finally completed by Rameses II. (Many scholars have held that Rameses was the biblical persecutor of the Hebrews.) The vast Hypostyle Hall was formed by adding seven rows of enormous columns to each side of Amenhotep's colonnaded avenue, making 134 columns in all, which were then covered with a roof and surrounded by a wall. The pillars and columns, which rise seventy-nine feet from the ground, are covered with reliefs depicting the exploits of the kings.

Decline of Amon's Cult, the Rise of a Monument

After the death of Rameses III around 1167 B.C., Thebes and Egypt went into decline, and the greatest era of monument building came to an end. However, during the Twenty-first Dynasty (ca. 1085–950 B.C.), the pharaohs assumed among their many titles that of chief priest of Amon-Re. As priest-kings of Thebes, they devoted some attention to the sanctuary of the god, but they were also intent on insuring their own authenticity. More for their own prestige than for the glory of Amon, the Libyan kings of the Twenty-second Dynasty (ca. 950–750 B.C.) constructed the masterful, pillared portico in the courtyard. Following their lead, Taharqua of the Ethiopian dynasty (ca. 750–665 B.C.) built a huge colonnade at the entrance to the temple. Through the second century A.D., the temples at Karnak were maintained and further decorated.

Though it was no longer a center of power, Thebes continued to be a place of sacred national memories. But in the course of centuries, the god Amon lost his

following to the rising powers of Christianity and of Islam. Karnak—with its many obelisks, pylons, and splendid temples—came to be inhabited by goats and later filled by desert sands.

It took an outsider, Napoleon Bonaparte, to rediscover the largely forgotten treasures at Karnak. When he landed in Egypt on July 2, 1798, he not only brought with him 38,000 soldiers but also a corps of nearly two hundred scientists and scholars in various fields. His experts eventually returned to Europe with the immortal Rosetta stone. Inscribed in three languages—Egyptian, Demotic, and Greek—the stone was the basis of the studies of the linguistic genius Jean François Champollion, who in 1822 finally deciphered the hieroglyphics of the ancient Egyptians. With this key, the study of Egyptology was born, and the Europeans began their scientific expeditions to recover the culture of the ancient pharaohs from the desert.

After centuries in the dust, the ruins of Amon's temple at Karnak are more than a rediscovered temple of a forgotten deity—they are a colossal and awe-inspiring monument to the glory of three thousand years of Egyptian civilization.

The Imperial Palace

Japan

Preceding page, the Kogosho, an audience hall of the Imperial Palace in Kyoto. Originally built in the thirteenth century, the Kogosho was used in the Middle Ages for formal audiences between emperors and their feudal lords and has been destroyed and rebuilt many times through the centuries. The rooms are designed to command a sweeping view of the adjacent large pond studded with tiny islands.

Left, three gates in the Imperial Compound, or Daidairi: above, an entrance with a gracefully curved roof; center, the Courtier's Gate in the western wall; and below, one of the entrances to the inner quarter.

Above, the Shishinden, a ceremonial audience hall, the largest and most formal building in the Kokyo—the residential section of the palace enclosure. The Shishinden is flanked by an orange tree symbolizing the spirit of Japan (right) and a cherry tree in bloom (left). The site of the emperor's coronation, it has a cypress roof and an eighteen-step entrance staircase. This is a nineteenth-century replica of the original.

Right, the steps of the Shishinden.

Left, the Ogakumonjo, or study, a building in the Kokyo containing six rooms, each with an alcove (tokonoma) for the display of hanging scrolls and flower arrangements.

Below left, the Serene and Cool Hall (Seiryoden), the emperor's residence within the Kokyo. The present building was reconstructed in 1855. The inner sections include a dining area; a room for the ritual purification which preceded the emperor's visits to shrines; and under the eastern eaves, the Hino-Goza, a place where official business was conducted.

Right, the eastern veranda of the Seiryoden. The main room of the building was called the moya. In the center is the micho, or emperor's throne.

Center, the Nagahashi, a passageway connecting the Shishinden (see page 125) to the Seiryoden. To the right is the screen on which the most important events of the year were recorded.

Below right, a view of the sliding, painted screens and shutters that provides contrast to the austere white walls of the palace interior.

Below, an intricate wooden window in the Tsunegoten, one of the emperor's residences.

Above left, a view of the white wall surrounding the Imperial Compound. Center, a Kyoto garden viewed through a gate. Right, a detail of a simple, yet elegant, stairway.

Below, a shuttered veranda extending from the Tsunegoten.

Facing page, a detail of a handsomely carved gable. The ornate roof decorations feature the chrysanthemum, one of the symbols of imperial Japan.

Several views of the gardens of Kyoto's Imperial Palace are shown on this page. The Japanese garden is designed to provide a tranquil setting for contemplation. It takes into account the changing colors according to the season, the constantly changing pattern of water in the ponds, and the relationships among trees and shrubs, rocks and moss. The prized qualities of wabi, *rustic solitude;* yugen, *tranquility; and* sabi, *the patina of age (as seen on moss-covered stones) suggest a timeless serenity. The garden re-creates nature in a "borrowed landscape" where all elements—plants, water, moss, and stones—are carefully arranged to achieve the most pleasing effect.*

Following page, another view of the Ogaku-monjo, showing the lake it faces and the decorative railing of a nearby bridge.

The Imperial Palace, Japan

"The water of a river flows constantly, today's water is no longer that of yesterday." This poetic statement, from a twelfth-century book of reflections by Kamo Chomei, describes an attitude toward the relationship between change and permanence that informs much of Japanese architecture. Perhaps it is this philosophic dimension that makes Japanese architecture so strange and intriguing to Westerners. To the Japanese, buildings are valued not so much for their material qualities as for their intrinsic symbolic meaning.

This philosophy is expressed in the singularly Japanese attitude toward simple stones. While a Westerner might value a stone for its structural properties, the Japanese have traditionally regarded stones as sacred objects, symbolizing longevity. So it is that the Japanese in their architecture have traditionally reserved stone mainly for footings at the base of wooden columns where they protect the column from rot and—equally important—provide symbolic protection for the building.

Yet the actual materials used in constructing palaces, temples, and residences—the untreated timber, the native clay plaster, the cedar shingles, the clay tiles—have been vulnerable to destruction and decay through the centuries. But this was not of paramount concern to the Japanese, who believe that it is always possible to replace, in effect regenerate, buildings—which reflect natural cycles of decay and renewal. Using traditional materials and techniques, the Japanese thus "recreate," rather than simply reconstruct, buildings that embody the essence of the originals. Many of the present buildings at Kyoto—even though they have been destroyed and rebuilt repeatedly—reflect the spirit and form of Japanese architectural patterns that were established over a thousand years ago.

Kyoto, the second imperial city of Japan, was founded in 792. Two years later, the emperor left the ancient capital

Below left, a stylized depiction of the Nijo Castle in Kyoto as it appears on an old screen. The castle was completed by Toyotomi Hideyoshi (ca. 1536–1598), a successful general in the army of Oda Nobunaga. Hideyoshi became the regent of Japan after Nobunaga's death. When Hideyoshi's successor, Tokugawa Ieyasu, moved Japan's capital to Tokyo in the early seventeenth century, he rebuilt Nijo Castle for regents visiting the older capital.

Above, a portrait of Oda Nobunaga (1534–1582), a feudal chief's son who fought his way to the position of de facto shogun.

of Nara, where there had been considerable political unrest. The emperor established his court at Kyoto, then called Heian-kyo, or Capital of Peace. Like Nara before it, the new city was laid out in a rectangle, following the plan of Chang-an, the capital of China during the Tang dynasty (618–907). The rectangle was originally subdivided into blocks that were symmetrically arranged along the central north-south axis. These blocks were defined by a network of streets that crisscrossed in a grid pattern. Surrounding the Imperial Compound, or Daidairi, were the homes of aristocrats and the more modest dwellings of the citizenry.

Most of the original buildings in the Imperial Compound—with their striking red pillars and blue tiled roofs—were modeled after Chinese prototypes. The Chinese practice of using fireproof clay tiles and lacquered wood was encouraged by Kammu, the founding emperor of Kyoto. However, the Chinese example never became very popular with the Japanese, who preferred untreated materials. In fact, as early as 724, the Council of State at the old capital at Nara had lamented that there were "still plank-roofed houses and thatched dwellings . . . difficult to build and easy to destroy." Neverthe-

less, later reconstructions allowed the Japanese to abandon tiled roofs and lacquered columns for the cypress shingles and natural wood construction we see today.

The imperial court knew nearly two hundred years of peace in the new capital at Kyoto before a fire destroyed the palace buildings in 960, signaling the first wave of a long cycle of destruction and reconstruction that has extended even to the present day. In 1192, a feudal military government, or shogunate, was established at Kamakura. From that time, the emperor, although still the symbolic head of state, had no real power, and the fortunes of Kyoto rose and fell at the whim of the feudal warlords and their samurai retainers. In the fourteenth century, Kyoto—no longer the "Capital of Peace" —was severely damaged in factional warfare. But by 1392, the Ashikaga dynasty of military rulers (shoguns) had re-established the center of government in Kyoto and rebuilt parts of the imperial city. However, factionalism and clan rivalry again plunged the country into bitter warfare, and by the end of the fifteenth century, Kyoto was virtually destroyed.

Nearly a century later, in 1568, Oda Nobunaga—a feudal lord who had united

Above, a woodcut showing the bank of the Tokyo River by Kitagawa Utamaro (1753–1806). This print shows a group of attractive women and children watching a fireworks display near the famous Ryogoku Bridge. By the eighteenth century, such middle-class pleasures had replaced the courtly pastimes of music, poetry, and moon-gazing.

most of the rival factions—took control of Kyoto and began to repair the imperial palaces. One of his more impressive projects was to begin construction of the fortified Nijo Castle, whose vast floors now extend harmoniously into gardens and courts.

Nobunaga was succeeded by Toyotomi Hideyoshi, who consolidated control of the country and was able to finally re-establish a national military government in Kyoto. Around 1590, Hideyoshi began to rebuild decaying palace buildings, and during the ensuing years of peace, he continued efforts to recapture Kyoto's former glory. Yet eighteen years after the death of Hideyoshi, the Tokugawa clan had gained control of the government and transferred the capital of the shogunate to Edo, now called Tokyo. Since that time Kyoto has assumed the role of the ceremonial and symbolic center of Japan.

The Imperial Compound

Japanese architecture and landscaping have evolved continually over the centuries, and their development is well represented in the many buildings of the Imperial Compound. An early type of building was the *shinden,* a series of pavilions connected by covered or enclosed walkways. Mainly a formal style used by the imperial court, it was derived from Chinese sources but constructed in the simple, natural materials favored by the Japanese. Also found at the Imperial

Below, a portrait of Toyotomi Hideyoshi, who united Japan in the sixteenth century after years of warfare.

Compound is the architectural type known as *shoin,* perhaps best known to Westerners in the form of the domestic Japanese dwelling. Unlike its predecessor, the *shinden*—with its arrangement of connecting pavilions—the *shoin* allows for all rooms in a single, compact structure. Inside, sliding partitions are used to define living spaces. Depending on need, the Japanese can divide their homes into several small areas or push all screens aside for uninterrupted space. The *shoin* is typically set off the ground on wood posts that enable the building to "flex" in the event of one of Japan's frequent earthquakes.

A third type of building, the *sukiya*—the tea ceremony room or house—reached a peak of refinement during the sixteenth and seventeenth centuries. The traditional

teahouse was small, with a thatched roof and plain plaster walls. The architectural simplicity of the teahouse corresponded to the spirit of the tea ritual, with its emphasis on asceticism and mental discipline. The small scale of the teahouse also accommodated intimate gatherings of friends who could drink tea while holding formal philosophic discussions.

The Imperial Palace, or Gosho—the palace complex within the Imperial Compound—consists of a configuration of pavilions in the *shinden* style. The Formal Audience Hall, or Shishinden, is along the same axis as the central gate of the Imperial Compound. In the center of the main room—with its satin-smooth floors—is a canopied dais, upon which the throne of

Above right and right, two depictions of Japanese theater. Above, illustration of an older theatrical form, the No play. The Western artist has vastly overestimated the size of the stage and has correspondingly dwarfed the actors. Kabuki (below) was a form of "open air" theater with music. Here it is presented for a lord and his samurai.

the emperor rests. Connected by a short, covered walkway is the Serene and Cool Hall, or Seiryoden, which was formerly the residence of the emperor but later reserved for ceremonial purposes. Though similar to the Shishinden in construction, it is subdivided into several smaller spaces suitable for an emperor's dwelling. To the northeast is the Kogosho, an audience hall from the feudal period, and nearby is the Ogakumonjo, which was used for formal meetings. The whole complex, which includes many other secondary buildings, is set into and surrounded by gardens, ponds, and dry landscapes.

To the Japanese, buildings not only have meaning unto themselves but also exist in an integral relationship with their natural surroundings. This correspondence between building and garden is achieved, in part, by the use of *shito-mido*—hinged "doors" that can be raised and hooked open—and *shoji*, which are sliding, paper-covered partitions. These exterior panels can be slid or swung open, removing any barriers between the Japanese home and the outside. In the past, the Japanese commonly slid partitions aside—even in the winter's cold—to afford unobstructed views of nature and its living symbol, the garden.

It is in the garden that the Japanese sensitivity to nature is perhaps most clearly revealed. Japanese gardens, with their clipped hedges, lanterns, tranquil ponds, and raked sand, are perceived as microcosms—small, enclosed representations of nature. In an environment of peace and serenity, the Japanese can stroll through their gardens, sometimes pausing to admire the dappled effect of light and shade on quiet ponds or stopping completely to contemplate the subtle movement of leaves in the breeze.

Today, visitors can walk through the Imperial Compound at Kyoto where the imperial buildings form part of an architectural continuum that stretches back to the earliest days of the ancient city. In

Above left, a woodcut of Sumo wrestling, an ancient and ritualized sport involving purification rites that give it a close connection to Shinto, Japan's ancient religion. The wrestlers—who belong to a heya, or gymnasium, run by former champions—weigh up to 350 pounds. Their combat is brief, rarely lasting more than thirty seconds, but involves a vast number of possible moves, attacks, holds, and throws. Sumo is preserved as pure sport; the Japanese never bet on the outcome of a match.

Above right, a woodcut by Katsushika Hokusai (1760–1849) showing a manually operated watermill, the type still seen occasionally in the countryside surrounding Kyoto.

1868, the government was moved to Tokyo, but the former capital city of Kyoto continues to be honored by the Japanese. Peasants still volunteer to work in the serene gardens surrounding the Imperial Palace in tribute to the ancient imperial order.

The Binnenhof

the Netherlands

Preceding page, an aerial view of the Binnenhof and Hofvijver, the rectangular lake which is its companion and complement. The thirteenth-century Hall of Knights (Ridderzaal) with its conically topped towers, occupies the central courtyard. Immediately behind it is the Hall of Rolls (Rolzaal).

Above, three views of the Binnenhof from the Hofvijver.

Right, equestrian statue of King William II at the entrance to the Binnenhof.

Far right, the beautiful Mauritshuis, built for Prince John Maurice of Nassau in the 1630s. Since 1816, the Mauritshuis has housed the Royal Museum of Painting.

Left, the courtyard of the Binnenhof as seen from the porch of the Hall of Knights.

The Hall of Knights fell into disuse during the eighteenth century, though subsequently used by Napoleon as a hospital and later used by the Dutch as archives. Restored at the end of the nineteenth century, it is now reserved for official state ceremonies.

Above and facing page, the Hall of Knights as seen from the courtyard of the Binnenhof.

Far left, details of the left-hand tower: the blacksmith figures which strike the hour and the decorative blind arches.

Left, details of the middle and lower part of the fountain that dominates the courtyard. The fountain is adorned with the coats of arms of the provinces of the Netherlands and is surmounted by a statue of Count William II.

Below, the rose window in the facade. In the center is the coat of arms of Queen Wilhelmina, in whose reign the Hall of Knights was restored, surrounded by the coats of arms of several other Dutch rulers.

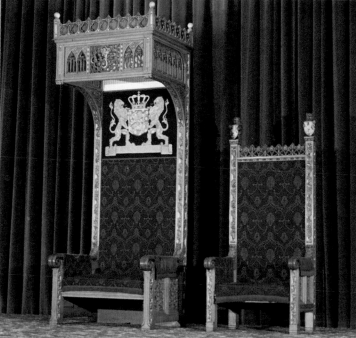

The Hall of Knights has been the site of many historic meetings of national and international significance, including the Second International Peace Conference in 1907, the first meeting of the Western European Union in 1947, the Round Table on the independence of Indonesia, and the declaration of equality between the Kingdom of the Netherlands and its excolonies in 1954.

The historic banners (above) of the eleven provinces that make up the Netherlands hang from the walls of the Hall of Knights. The queen opens the States-General in the Hall of Knights each year.

Left, the throne of the queen and her consort.

Above, the canopied throne formerly used by Dutch monarchs.

Right, two views of the Hall of the Truce (Treveszaal), whose name commemorates an early seventeenth-century truce in Holland's wars of independence with Spain. Designed by the French architect Daniel Marot, it was built in the last years of the seventeenth century. It is an excellent example of the grand Louis XIV style. Its ceiling is picturesquely supported by twelve hermes and caryatids. The great oval fresco, the work of Theodor van der Schmeer, represents the apotheosis of the Dutch state.

Left, top to bottom: the staircase of the Mauritshuis, a building adjacent to the Binnenhof; the Lairesse Chamber, named after the painter who decorated it in the seventeenth century; the old kitchens, now a waiting room for visitors to the Hall of Knights.

Above right, the fine ornamentation of the Princess's Chamber, so called in honor of Wilhelmina of Prussia, wife of William V.

Right, detail of a woodcarving along a banister and (far right) a detail of the restored fireplace in the Hall of the Tribunal. The coats of arms reflect a time when Holland was among the dominions of the dukes of Burgundy.

Following page, a view of the Binnenhof from across the Hofvijver.

The Binnenhof, the Netherlands

When Louis XIV of France transferred his capital from Paris to Versailles and established his court and government in a palace in an open park rather than in a fortified castle, it was a visible testimony to the supreme confidence of the Sun King. After all, only a truly mighty sovereign could discount the need for walls, towers, and other defensive structures and could rely entirely on his soldiers for his personal safety and protection.

But ironically, the citizens of the Netherlands—whom the Sun King despised for refusing to bow down to his might—had built a capital without walls nearly a century earlier. The Hague had no conventional fortifications. In fact, the canals constructed between 1613 and 1619 by Prince John Maurice of Nassau were the only available defenses for the political center of a country whose citizens habitually shouted, "Open the dikes!" at the first sign of invaders.

In the late Middle Ages, the Netherlands had been linked to France, Germany, and England by politics and trade, but as early as the twelfth and thirteenth centuries, it began to grow as an independent region. In the south, the Flemish cloth merchants emerged as leaders in European commerce. But life was harder on the North Sea coast of the province of Holland, where the sea was a constant threat and the land was poor. According to one Arab traveler, the site where The Hague was later built was no more than an unpromising stretch of flat land, lashed by winds and flooded by the sea.

In 1579, seven provinces—Gelderland, Holland, Zeeland, Utrecht, Friesland, Overijssel, and Groningen—signed the Union of Utrecht and established a loose federation known as the United Provinces, or the Dutch Republic. They established their federal parliament, the States-General, in The Hague and designated William the Silent, a count of Holland, as the first stadholder (chief magistrate).

But by the time of the Union of Utrecht, the province of Holland had the richest and largest towns, the greatest fleets, and the largest population. Throughout Europe, "Hollander" was becoming synonymous with "Netherlander." Under these circumstances, it was only natural that a town in the province of Holland should eventually become the capital of the United Provinces.

The Hague had perhaps twenty or thirty thousand inhabitants at the end of the sixteenth century, but it did not officially become a city until the time of Napoleon. Francesco Guicciardini—a Florentine politician, diplomat, and contemporary of Machiavelli—once quipped that The Hague was "the most important village in Europe." His description is still quoted approvingly, not only in guidebooks but also by the Dutch themselves.

Below, the Hall of Knights, identified here as "de Groote Saalle" (Great Hall), probably its original name. This seventeenth-century print depicts the execution of Jan van Oldenbarnevelt, a statesman, beheaded as a religious heretic in 1619.

"The Count's Hedge"

The feudal counts of Holland—who were the predecessors of William the Silent—were not the newest aristocrats in the Holy Roman Empire, but neither were they the most established. To help consolidate their power, Count William I (1203–1222) became a leader in the series of cooperative efforts between the territorial units of the Netherlands. It was William who founded the Waterschapen, the system of local water control authorities whose existence would eventually lead to the development of a decentralized but highly organized Holland of the seventeenth century. His grandson, William II, was no less concerned with the problems of consolidation, especially since he had far-reaching political ambitions. After inheriting the title of count of Holland in 1234, he was later nominated as a claimant to the title of Holy Roman Emperor.

Though William II's imperial ambitions were never realized, his claim to the throne made him the most influential aristocrat in the Netherlands, and he decided to construct a residence that would be an appropriate reflection of this new-found power. William selected a site several miles north of the mouth of the Rhine, where running water flowed down from the surrounding dunes.

Here William cleared a stretch of untouched land and enclosed the area with walls and canals. The enclosure came to be called 's-Gravenhage, which literally means "the count's hedge." And in time, it became known simply as Den Haag, or the hedge, from which the English derived The Hague.

Inner Court of Power

The massive residential hall that William built within this enclosure, completed in 1248, was the original building of both The Hague and the Binnenhof. William died before he could fully establish his *hof* (court), but his son and successor, Count Floris V, continued his father's plans by constructing the Hall of Knights (Ridderzaal), also called the Grand Hall.

The Hall of Knights stands at the center of the large rectangular complex known as the Binnenhof, which means the "inner court." Completed in 1280, the Hall of Knights made the Binnenhof the permanent seat of power for the counts of Holland as well as for subsequent rulers of the Netherlands. Even today, the restored Hall of Knights remains the architectural and symbolic focus of the Binnenhof.

Several elements of the Hall of Knights are reminiscent of the religious architecture of the late Middle Ages. One example of such a motif is the towers flanking the southwestern façade. These slender towers are elegant, stylized allusions to the spires of the great German imperial cathedrals. Both the towers and the Hall of Knights

Left, two eighteenth-century views of the inner courtyard of the Binnenhof, showing the Hall of Knights before its restoration.

have undergone alterations and restorations over the centuries, but their austere, Dutch Gothic character has been well preserved. Restoration has fortunately been confined to a faithful reproduction of the original features, especially the timber-beamed ceiling of the hall.

Hall of Rolls

Directly behind the Hall of Knights is the Hall of Rolls (Rolzaal), which is on the site of William II's original building dating from the mid-thirteenth century. It was rebuilt in the early sixteenth century and transformed into a law court, where the "rolls"—listing the names of those whose cases would be tried—were read before the court. It was in the Hall of Rolls that Jan van Oldenbarnevelt was convicted of religious heresy and sentenced to death in 1619, after having served the Dutch state for over forty years. Today, the hall still serves a ceremonial function during the annual meeting of the States-General at the Binnenhof.

Surprisingly enough, the original medieval complex was much larger than the present-day Binnenhof. The former main entrance gate, the Prisoner's Gate (Gevangenpoort) now lies well outside the present boundaries of the Binnenhof. The fifteenth-century bulk of the Prisoner's Gate stands between what used to be the old Buitenhof, now the central square of The Hague, and the new Plaats, which in other times was known as the Green Sward, where prisoners of the state were executed.

In the middle of the Plaats, the statue of Jan de Witt looks down on the scene of his death. Appointed pensionary of Holland by the States-General in 1653, de Witt pursued a successful foreign policy with the hostile English and French and defended the independence of the Netherlands against their threats for nearly twenty years.

Unfortunately, the princes of Orange who had been refused the title of stad-

Above, the departure of William V of Orange, who was forced to flee to England on January 18, 1795, when the Batavian Republic was established by the French as a sister republic.

Right, an eighteenth-century meeting of the States-General in the Binnenhof.

holder by the States-General were to become Jan de Witt's bitter rivals, jealous of his political success.

In 1672, the military successes of William III of Orange against the French enabled him to gather enough popular support to reclaim the stadholder title that he believed was his by hereditary right. On August 20, 1672, Jan de Witt was imprisoned in the Prisoner's Gate. His brother Cornelius had already been tortured there and was soon to die. Jan de Witt himself

died at the hands of an Orangist mob who dragged him from the prison and killed him not far from the States-General, the scene of many of de Witt's previous personal and political triumphs. William III, the new master of the Binnenhof, made only a perfunctory effort to find the murderers of Jan de Witt and bring them to justice.

The Binnenhof at the time of William of Orange was a very different place from the residence of the old counts of Holland.

Below, the Hall of Knights in the eighteenth century.

Left, a nineteenth-century impression. The changes and alterations that have occurred in the interim are clearly visible: Certain structures have been demolished, and the lower part of the façade restored, though it has not yet reached its final—and presumably original—configuration (see page 143).

There had been a period of disuse and decay during the sixteenth century, when the emperor Charles V—sovereign of an empire upon which, he was fond of saying, the sun never set—disliked the old Binnenhof and commissioned his architects to build a new royal palace elsewhere.

In 1644, Jacob van Campen completed the Mauritshuis, which stands in the northeast corner of the Hofvijver—a small rectangular lake that was formed by enlarging a canal. An elegant Palladian villa, it was built for Prince John Maurice of Nassau, who had been governor of Brazil for the Dutch West India Company. The Mauritshuis is a fine example of seventeenth-century Dutch classicism. Like the Binnenhof, it overlooks the Hofvijver. Today, the Mauritshuis houses the Royal Museum of Painting, one of the most important Dutch galleries. In the past, it was the scene of several critical events in Dutch political history, including the signing of the Act of Abjuration on July 24, 1581. In this document, the representatives of Holland, the Brabant, Flanders, Utrecht, Gelderland, and Zeeland, all under William the Silent, renounced their allegiance to Phillip II, the king of Spain.

During the seventeenth and eighteenth centuries, the late-medieval buildings of the Binnenhof were gradually replaced by classical buildings, and painters and architects came from all parts of Europe to adorn and enrich the seat of the States-General of the Netherlands. Daniel Marot, a Huguenot whom Louis XIV had forced into religious exile, designed the Assembly of the States-General and the famous Hall of the Truce (Treveszaal)—so named to commemorate the Treaty of Rijswik, which had brought a short truce to the wars between Spain and the Dutch under Prince Maurice. Built between 1696 and 1698, it is perhaps the finest of all the public rooms in the Binnenhof. Its Louis XIV-style decorations have been preserved perfectly.

Certainly, the Hall of the Truce is a greater achievement than either of the other formal assembly rooms: the mid-seventeenth-century Senate Hall (the Eerste Kamer)—once the ancient hall of the States-General—and the Chamber of Deputies (Tweede Kamer), which was converted from an elegant, eighteenth-century ballroom.

Today, the States-General still holds its sessions in The Hague, and the Hall of Knights is the ceremonial throne room of the Netherlands. Here, the two chambers of the States-General stand before the queen and her ministers. They represent a people who throughout seven hundred years of struggle have had to protect their country from the ceaseless threats of the sea. There is a saying: "God made the sea, the Dutch made the land." The Dutch have also preserved their way of life on a small piece of land more densely populated than the Ganges Delta.

The Dutch are considered to be among the most civilized and most tolerant people in the world. And on ceremonial occasions at the Hall of Knights, it is easy to recognize their respect for tradition. Much was implied by the pledge of William the Silent, which his descendants have adopted as their motto: *Je maintiendrai* (I shall maintain). His words have come to symbolize all that has been gained by the pride and tenacity of a people who have transformed a small, unremarkable clearing into a capital city and a feudal castle into the symbol of a free republic.

Edinburgh Castle

Scotland

Preceding page, the ancient buildings of Edinburgh Castle seen from the eighteenth-century New Town in the soft, early light of a summer morning.

Facing page, the castle as seen from the Old Town.

Right and below left, the castle entrance. After a broad esplanade, there is a bridge across the moat leading to a compact wall that is broken only by two niches and the stone coat of arms on the guardhouse. Finally, there is a long rise between the walls to the Portcullis Gate (below right) beneath the National War Memorial. Such are the barriers to be overcome to gain the heart of the fortress.

Above and left, the northeast corner of the palace and a view (facing page, above right) of the façade overlooking the courtyard. In this building is Mary Queen of Scots's room, a small chamber that has been heavily restored. This wing was considerably altered between 1615 and 1617 and is a fine example of sixteenth- and seventeenth-century architecture in Scottish Renaissance style. The royal residence is completed by the Great Hall, which stands at right angles to the main building and faces south.

Far right, Mons Meg, the prized gun of the Scots, seen in the distance. An imposing national relic, it is made of massive iron bars, held together by metal rings. To its left is St. Margaret's Chapel.

Center right, the chapel of the National War Memorial, built in 1927 on the site of an ancient church.

Right, the nineteenth-century hospital, built in the National Romantic "Scottish Baronial" style, which occupies the site of the old powder magazine.

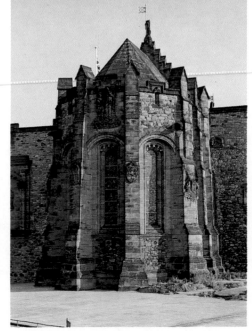

Because the castle is both a fortress and a national monument, the severe utility of the buildings has in many cases been softened by decorative details, such as in the niches (left and below left) that are set into the walls of the National War Memorial. The theme of these decorations is nearly always martial.

Facing page, the martial symbol of lion and shield.

Above, one of the many heraldic monuments which commemorates the castle's association with great generals and statesmen. This stone celebrates the heroism of Thomas Randolph, the earl of Moray, who defeated the English in 1313 and took Edinburgh Castle in the name of his uncle Robert the Bruce, then king of Scotland.

The ceiling of the apse of the National War Memorial Chapel (left) with its sober and evocative lines, contrasts with the upper floors of a small building (above) where the most heterogeneous architectural forms are assembled with great imagination.

Above, the Great Hall. The massive beams of the ceiling are embellished with carvings of human and animal heads, which are fine examples of early Renaissance work in Scotland. The room, once used for royal banquets and receptions, now houses a collection of weapons and armor.

Left, two ornamental doorways at the castle. The doorway on the right is at the entrance to the hospital and shows symbols traditionally associated with medicine.

Following page, the castle as seen from the graveyard of Edinburgh's West Kirk, the city's oldest church.

Edinburgh Castle, Scotland

The sensational stories of intrigue, warfare, and suffering associated with Edinburgh Castle would almost seem excessive if incorporated into a historical novel. From the Middle Ages through the eighteenth century, the castle played a major role in the never-ending conflicts among Scotland's rival clans and her long series of wars with England. Consequently, Edinburgh Castle was the scene of terrible sieges, plunder, murder, imprisonment, and exile, and it served variously as a fortress, treasure house, and national religious shrine.

The cycle of destruction and restoration that the castle has endured over many centuries has resulted in an amalgam of architectural forms. The castle's oldest surviving structure preserves the tradition of Norman architecture. Other buildings dating back to the sixteenth century are fine examples of architecture from the Scottish Renaissance. The remaining parts of the castle are more modern reconstructions, evoking the spirit of the many original buildings that were destroyed during the long history of Edinburgh Castle.

The prehistoric origins of the castle add a rich resonance to its later history. The ancient Picts and Celts, who first settled on the rocky bluff at the mouth of the Forth River as long ago as the Bronze Age, left a legacy of colorful legends and ghosts to an already picturesque site. The castle stands on an outcrop, rising 443 feet above a landscape of marshes, forests, and pasture land. The Castle Rock was also the site of a Roman fort in the first century. In the sixth century, when Saint Columba came from Ireland to convert the Scots from their ancient pagan religion, he established an early Christian community where the castle now stands.

The earliest reliable information about Edinburgh Castle dates from the eleventh century, the time of Malcolm III (1058–1093). After Malcolm reclaimed the Scottish throne from a usurper who had murdered his father King Duncan, Edinburgh became the seat of the Scottish monarchy. The events of this distant era, mingled with Celtic mythology, witchcraft, and druidic legends of the forest, were immortalized by Shakespeare in the great tragedy *Macbeth*.

It was Malcolm's wife Queen Margaret, widely respected for her cultured and refined tastes, who began to turn the austere fortress at Edinburgh into a more comfortable royal residence. Unfortunately, the finely woven tapestries and paneled walls of Margaret's private rooms have long been destroyed.

A popular and saintly queen who was later canonized, Margaret built a small chapel where she was "wont to spend much of her time in prayer" and where she is said to have venerated a fragment of the true cross. The tiny Norman chapel—the

Below, Mary Stuart and her third husband, the earl of Bothwell. This portrait of Bothwell is based on his mummified remains.

Bottom, the monogram of Mary Stuart and Lord Darnley, decorating the entrance to their royal apartments.

Left, a sixteenth-century view of Edinburgh and its castle as they looked in Mary's time.

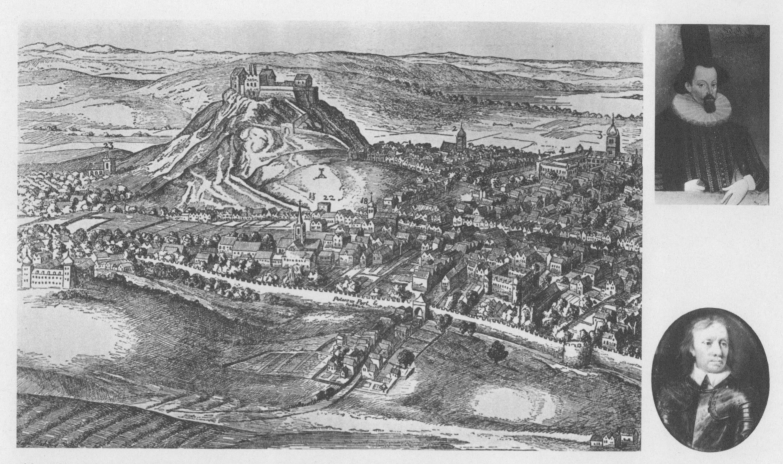

oldest church in Scotland—can still be seen today at the uppermost part of the castle. Built in the local freestone, it has a small, semicircular apse framed by a massive arch that is carved with elaborate geometric designs. In 1853, it was thoroughly restored at the order of Queen Victoria after centuries of deconsecration—for a time, it had even served as a warehouse.

In 1174, Edinburgh Castle was occupied by the English after Henry II defeated and captured William the Lion (1165–1214) at Alnwick. The castle was part of a heavy ransom the Scots paid to have William the Lion released. However, the castle was returned to the Scots after William bought back the independence of his country from Henry II's son, Richard the Lion-Hearted, who was raising money for the Third Crusade.

The castle was an important center of Scottish nationalism during the reign of Alexander III (1244–1286). Nevertheless, his wife Margaret, daughter of Henry III of England, could not have found it a very congenial place to live. In her melancholy words, the castle was "sad and lonely, treeless and unhealthy because it is so near the sea...."

Curiously, her description was prophetic of the turmoil and upset associated with the castle following the death of her husband. A dispute over the succession to the Scottish throne gave Edward I of England an excuse to order the removal of the Scottish crown jewels housed at Edinburgh for "safekeeping" until a new monarch was named. But even after Edward himself named John Baliol king of Scotland, the valuables were not restored to Edinburgh. In fact, they were not returned for another 150 years, not until after the Wars of Independence.

The English once more occupied Edinburgh after an eight-day siege when John Baliol revolted against his feudal lord, Edward I, and lost. The castle was again reconquered for the Scots in 1313 by the earl of Moray, a nephew of Robert the Bruce, the popular, newly crowned king of Scotland. By the new king's command, the castle and its fortifications were totally destroyed, except for St. Margaret's Chapel, so that Edinburgh Castle would never again be a vantage point from which the English could subjugate the Scottish countryside.

Despite Robert the Bruce's desperate

Above left, Edinburgh Castle as depicted in a seventeenth-century print. During that century the castle was the scene of the coronation of James VI (top) and of the siege in 1650 by Cromwell (immediately above).

Below, the castle displayed on the great seal of Edinburgh.

precautionary measures, the English occupied Edinburgh again during the time of his son, David II (1329–1371), and their garrison began to restore the fortress. The fortress was recaptured by the Scots, and when David II returned from his English imprisonment, he began restoration work of his own. King David's Tower, as it was known, took ten years to build. In 1913, it was discovered that parts of King David's Tower still remain, incorporated in the Half-Moon Battery of 1574.

The Stuart Dynasty: The King's Lodging and the Great Hall

When David died in 1371, leaving no direct heir, the throne passed to the ill-fated Stuarts (originally Stewart, from the hereditary office long held by this family of stewards to the royal household). Under the Stuarts, a series of improvements transformed Edinburgh into a proper royal palace. Meanwhile, the quarrels of the Scottish aristocracy and the wars and skirmishes with the English continued. Edinburgh Castle, rarely the seat of powerful monarchs, was more often a refuge for sovereigns in disgrace—as frequently a prison for the unfortunate sovereigns as for their enemies.

Robert II (1371–1390), the first Stuart king, allowed the burgesses of Edinburgh to build houses within the castle walls for protection in periods of war. During the time of his great-grandson James II (1437–1460), a vendetta between the Stuarts and the Douglases was precipitated by the "Black Dinner" murders. In this treacherous episode, James II first honored, then murdered, the earl of Douglas and his younger brother in the castle banquet hall. The outcome of James II's daring foul play was a nine-month siege during which most of the castle was destroyed and James II was killed. James III (1460–1488), however, rebuilt the castle. He also imprisoned his own brother Alexander, duke of Albany, in King David's Tower because of suspicions of

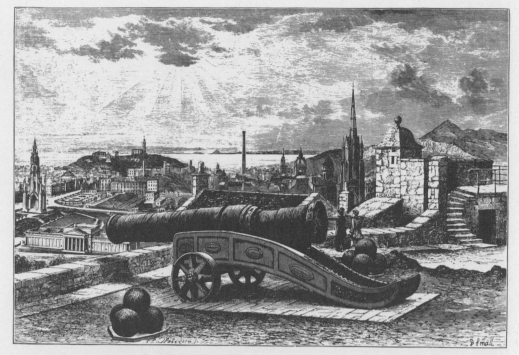

Above, Mons Meg, an enormous, fifteenth-century cannon which burst while firing a birthday salute to the duke of York in 1682.

Left, St. Margaret's Chapel, where the sainted queen is said to have worshipped a fragment of the true cross.

Alexander's intrigues with England and his popularity among the Scots. The English king eventually interceded in the duke of Albany's behalf, and James III himself spent several months in the tower. The reign of James IV (1488–1513) spanned an idyllic interlude in the otherwise grim history of Edinburgh Castle. Allied with the English through his marriage to Henry VII's daughter Margaret Tudor, he was also a relatively strong king at home. James IV lived in the nearby Holyrood Palace, but he frequently used Edinburgh Castle to stage jousting tournaments and revels. He commissioned the architect Sir James Hamilton to redesign the royal accommodations at Edinburgh, and the Great Hall and the King's Lodging were

also constructed.

Relations with the English were strained once again when Henry VIII became king of England because James IV persisted in his devout Catholicism and in a friendship with the French. James and many Scottish peers were killed in a battle against the English in 1512. As a result of the continuing tensions with England, the next king, James V, built a foundry at Edinburgh that turned out some of the finest artillery in Europe. Ironically, he was mortally wounded by English artillery in a battle in 1542. His widow Mary of Guise continued to rule Scotland to insure the succession of their daughter Mary Stuart, who was only a week old when James died. This infant grew up to be the

Left, Edinburgh as depicted in a nineteenth-century print. Its appearance has since changed greatly, but the mighty castle still dominates the city.

throne of his ancestors. It was somewhat of an uninspired siege, with unwilling defenders opposing ill-equipped assailants. Neither of the opponents had any idea of the strength (or weakness) of the other, and after a few days, the Young Pretender moved off to Holyrood, where he held court for a time before beginning an audacious, but ultimately unsuccessful, campaign against the English.

During the eighteenth century, the strategic importance of the castle gradually declined, though it did continue to serve as a minor barracks and as a prison.

Edinburgh Castle has undergone many alterations in its long history as a fortress and venerated shrine. What was once a turreted medieval castle is now a picturesque assortment of more recent buildings—a hospital, barracks, palace, governor's house, and National War Monument. Of the most ancient castle, only the restored Chapel of St. Margaret in the uppermost Citadel still remains as the historic and symbolic heart of the imposing fortress.

The castle is still surrounded by massive walls which support the Half-Moon Battery and the Portcullis Gate—the sole entrance to the fortress and one of its grandest features. The castle esplanade—parade ground of the garrison for centuries—was redesigned in the nineteenth century and continues to be the scene of the traditional pageantry of Scottish pipe and drum tattoos. The Great Hall on the south side of the Palace Yard now houses the United Services Museum, which contains a valuable collection of weapons and armor.

The crown, scepter, and sword of Scotland are displayed in the vaulted Crown Room of the palace. But more than these "Honors of Scotland," as the ancient regalia of the Scottish monarchs are called, Edinburgh Castle itself is a symbol of Scotland's fierce and turbulent past and of its unique cultural heritage. Its austere walls, which have risen above so much blood and destruction, are a monument to the uncompromising pride and nationalistic spirit of the Scots.

tragic Mary Queen of Scots.

- Mary Stuart was raised for the most part in France, and she first visited Edinburgh Castle in 1561 as the heir to the throne. (Her mother had died in 1560.) Her son, who was to become James VI of Scotland and James I of England, was born in Edinburgh Castle in 1567. Shortly after her second husband, Lord Darnley, was murdered, the earl of Bothwell—who was chief suspect in the murder—married the queen. The marriage troubled her subjects, who suspected Mary of being a murderous adultress. Mary was eventually forced to abdicate in favor of her son James. She was imprisoned for a short time at Edinburgh before being removed to the island fortress of Lochleven.

On her abdication, Mary appointed one of her most faithful followers, Sir William Kirkaldy of Grange, as commandant of the castle. In 1571, Sir William received money and arms from the French—turning previous rumors of his treachery to fact. The situation dragged on indecisively until 1573, when Elizabeth I sent troops and artillery into Edinburgh. The siege lasted for more than a month, and much of the castle, including King David's Tower, was destroyed by cannon fire. When the rebels surrendered, Sir William

was promptly hanged. A stone set in the walls now commemorates the siege and Sir William's execution.

While James VI never visited Edinburgh as king, he spent significant sums on its upkeep and commissioned considerable building and restoration around 1615. Charles I spent one night at Edinburgh before his coronation in 1633, and Charles II also lodged there briefly in 1650. Thereafter, no king entered the castle until the reign of George IV in the nineteenth century.

The castle had remained an important fortress, however, and was the scene of several nationalistic conflicts. It was a stronghold for the Scottish forces loyal to the English king during the English Civil War, and Cromwell bombarded it for three months before successfully occupying it in 1650. The last great siege occurred during the Glorious Revolution of 1688, which deposed the Catholic James II, who was the last Stuart king, in favor of the Protestants Mary II and William III of Orange. The siege lasted three months, and in the end, the duke of Gordon took the castle. A less distinguished, yet historically noteworthy, attack on Edinburgh occurred in 1745 when Bonnie Prince Charlie arrived from France to claim the